I0095007

How Not to Hate Advertising

Written by an award-winning Chief Creative Officer (CCO) and featuring insights from agency and freelance advertising pros, this book is the creative professionals' guidebook, self-help book, and halftime speech/pep talk book all wrapped up in one. It's written for working creatives to help them sustain and succeed in an industry that has plenty to hate about it.

This is not a "how to break into the business" book, and it doesn't aim to explain the creative process and how to come up with ideas. Instead, it accepts and expects that the reader has already done the hard part of breaking in and (hopefully) getting some work produced that they're proud of – it's the "what's next" to avoid burnout, filled with practical tips, sage advice, and real stories from an array of people who have definitely hated advertising at some point – but stuck with it anyway.

A sort of treasure map that creatives can use to guide them through different stages of their career, this book is pure gold for advertising professionals and students who want to thrive in their chosen industry while taking care of their whole selves, now and into the future.

Nick Sonderup is an award-winning creative leader with 23+ years of experience. His work has been recognized by nearly every industry awards show, including Cannes Lions, ANDYs, One Show, Clio, Effies, D&AD, and the ADC. His work for General Electric earned an Emmy nomination, and his film *100 Bands in 100 Days* was a Grand Jury award nominee at the 2010 SXSW Film Festival. Nick is currently Co-CCO at StrawberryFrog, responsible for leadership across multiple accounts, the creative department, and the StrawberryFrog brand. Over the years, Nick has lent his expertise to a broad range of brands, including MTV, ESPN, American Express, MINI, AT&T, Nike, Anheuser-Busch InBev, State Farm, Midea, Northwell Health, and more. He also created powerful, soulful work at many of the industry's most celebrated creative agencies, like Wieden+Kennedy (W+K), BBDO, Ogilvy, and Translation, after starting his career at MTV. Outside of agency life, Nick has worked as an Adjunct Professor teaching copywriting.

How Not to Hate Advertising

A Creative's Guide to a Long and (Dare I Say) Happy Career in a Remarkably Silly Industry

Nick Sonderup

Routledge
Taylor & Francis Group
NEW YORK AND LONDON

Designed cover image: Bryan Haker

First published 2026
by Routledge
605 Third Avenue, New York, NY 10158

and by Routledge
4 Park Square, Milton Park, Abingdon, Oxon, OX14 4RN

Routledge is an imprint of the Taylor & Francis Group, an informa business

For Product Safety Concerns and Information please contact our EU representative GPSR@taylorandfrancis.com. Taylor & Francis Verlag GmbH, Kaufingerstraße 24, 80331 München, Germany.

ISBN: 9781032615684 (hbk)
ISBN: 9781032615646 (pbk)
ISBN: 9781032615707 (ebk)

DOI: 10.4324/9781032615707

Typeset in Galliard
by codeMantra

Dedicated to my wife, Sunshine Flint, who has listened to me complain about my job more than anyone on earth should have to. And my twin daughters, Evelyn and Persephone, who actually love to watch commercials – not just mine.

HATERS GONNA HATE

Designer: Bryan Haker.

Contents

Foreword

Jeff Kling

Jeff Kling. CCO/Founder, Das Favorite.

"How Not To Hate Advertising"

CIVILIANS: WUT. Why tf would anyone want to do that?

PEOPLE RESPONSIBLE FOR THINGS THAT GET LOGOS: Lemme make some popcorn.

People – of which people in advertising are a constituent subset – people hate advertising. This will surprise no one who has ever seen advertising. Advertising is stupid. The wrong kind. People want it like they want botched daily root canal surgery, performed with a fork, by strong, unclean hands. That people hate advertising is as just, correct, and deserved as snap, crackle, pop.

It's not much better for the people who make ads (content, logoed things, branded entertainment, wearables, please stop). For starters, people who make ads are also people, so unless they're delusional, people who make ads also hate it. But then they also have to live with making it. Which is doubly hateful. Many of them – and any unlikely civilian readers of a book by this title will scarcely credit it as possible, given advertising's output – many people who make advertising are trying, really trying, against staggering headwinds, to make branded things the public (and they themselves) don't hate. It's Sisyphus work. It would be easier to fit a boring but loud camel through the eye of an inane but unavoidable needle.

And yet.

If I could attribute the following idea I would, as some anonymous-to-me genius said something like it, nailing the nature of advertising: People hate advertising generally but love it specifically.

Ask one hundred people anywhere on planet earth if they like advertising, one hundred and one of them will say HELL no. But alter the prompt slightly – "Tell us about an ad you've seen recently that you like" – and nearly every person will light up like a pinball machine, eyeballs extending temporarily four inches beyond their resting sockets, and say: Oh, yeah! There's that one with the guy, who says that thing! And that other one, with the monkey in college, et cetera.

At a species level we hate advertising, categorically, but almost everyone at all times has in mind a particular thing she/they/he doesn't hate.

Hope!

Some things get through! Some appallingly low percentage of logoed things do cut through, and write their names on public hearts. They become culture, even. We can look back on them decades later through nostalgia's Vaselined lens, and we do not hate the resulting, if distorted, self-portrait.

Why the industry so woefully, systemically misses is a subject for a different book, and the motivating premise of my own agency, dedicated to making logoed things people love: Das Favorite.

Crucially:

Lest anyone in the dark communication and connection arts feels too isolated in her/his/their professional self-loathing, and lest the gen pop gets too comfy in smug superiority: everybody advertises. Everybody. Every. Single. Gattam. Human. On. This. Browning. Earth. Advertises.

Everyone.

The kid showing mom how almost totally clean his dinner plate is. Abuela giving a tour of her new living facility to the hijos – This is where I get to meet and play dominoes with all my friends; this is the marvelous dining room where they serve us any delicious thing we could ask for – practically quoting its website. Your friend saying, "C'mon," "It'll be fun," and "It's only a freestyle root canal. With a specialized fork."

I shamelessly plugged my own enterprise not four paragraphs ago.

Everyone's got something to sell, something to merchandise, some point to make, some thing of which you absolutely must be convinced. Here, at the exciting post-democratic finalé of our capitalist experiment, we encode that everybody advertises in phrases like "I buy that" and "I don't buy that" to express being (un)convinced. Whether you're *sold* on that – you get the point.

Everyone advertises. No one gets out alive.

So. How do we not hate the advertising we all do?

Lord knows: in every human endeavor, when we're not having fun, it shows.

I'm guessing Nick has some solid, helpful ideas. He's been at this ad thing a minute; he cares so sincerely to make a dent in our hate ratios that he wrote a whole book.

The citizenry needs someone throwing energy into helping others find joy in this scarcely legitimate field – to the benefit of its output, to the benefit of the public exposed to that output, and for the pleasure of insatiable deity Mammon, upon whose satisfaction so much depends.

The New York Times just published a cheery article claiming we can put all the creative wizardry we want into our eyes, hands, and ears, but by the time the period dries at the end of this book, everything will have shifted again, and planet-scorching bots will have made another non-trivial chunk of people redundant.

Is humanity replaceable?

Is your humanity replaceable?

Can a bot replicate your voice because your voice lacks distinction?

Put yourself in your work and it will be relatably, appealingly human. Or as Stacy Wall once told me with enviable crispiness: put what you love into your work and your work will be lovable.

Advertising is an industry of mostly good people doing mostly bad things.

It doesn't have to be that way. Our days and output needn't be as hateful as they are.

Each of us can make that difference. That difference is on nobody but us.

Lift it, shift it.

Beep boop.

A note on hate

The word hate will be used a lot throughout this book. You've probably seen it like ten times already at this point, provided you read the cover, the spine, the Foreword, this sentence, and the heading above it. If you didn't, what's up? I thought we were cool?

Hate is a terrible thing. A dirty word. A dark notion. But in this context, it's really just another way of saying love. To not hate is to love. Or at least to like. Or tolerate. Or be fine with. Or whatever. This is not to diminish the true nature of all horrible things in this world the word 'hate' applies to, like hate speech, hate groups, hate crimes, hate-watching cable news when you should be sleeping…you get the gist.

I know you're smart enough to figure all of this out, so don't hate me for overexplaining it. But I would hate for there to be any misunderstanding.

Courtesy of Wieden + Kennedy, London.

Preface

At the time I set out to write this book, my career was in a different place. I was the Executive Creative Director (ECD) of a mid-sized New York agency, leading creative and co-leading the office. In my tenure, we'd won a lot of new business, grew existing business, won a bunch of awards, and snagged PR headlines, inside and outside the industry. Life was good. For me, this position was the culmination of a 20+ year career of hard work, grinding it out at different creative agencies (W+K, BBDO, Translation, Ogilvy) and one in-house creative department (MTV). There were many battles won and lost, weight lost and gained, friendships and relationships fostered, and countless productions and pitches in the win and loss columns.

Then suddenly, it ended.

I'd become another casualty of a volatile business in uncertain times. I wasn't alone, but it certainly felt like it. This was my first time getting laid off, which from what I'm told is kind of amazing after 20 years. But it didn't feel amazing. It was numbing. Everything came to a grinding halt. The emails. The Gchats. The fire drills. The complaints from Account about some pain in the ass CD. The complaints from a CD about a pain in the ass Account person. Silence. That was the most jarring part. I was so used to being needed all the time. Now all I had was time, and no one needed me anymore. Advertising was moving on. Talk about a reason to hate what you do for a living, right?

But I didn't. Ok, maybe for a few weeks I did, but I got over it. After decades of extreme highs and lows, I didn't and still don't hate advertising. I don't always love it, but I wouldn't use the word hate. Has it used me? Yes. Abused me? At times. Has it rewarded me beyond my wildest expectations, financially and creatively? You bet. Has it defeated me? Not yet. And it doesn't have to defeat you, either.

I never thought I'd be writing a book about not hating advertising, after being chewed up and spit out by advertising. At least that's how it felt at the time. But the great thing about advertising is that things can change as quickly for you as they do for the industry. Over a year has passed and I'm back in a full-time role as Co-CCO at StrawberryFrog, an independent creative agency. The one thing that hasn't changed is my belief in the business. No matter how many people try to declare the death of advertising, or that things will never be the same – I declare, it's still a business that runs on ideas. And I love ideas.

And I'm more appreciative than ever before, for the chance to dream up big, dumb ideas, most of which will never get made. Or the chance to grind out a final pitch deck. Or sit in traffic for two hours to attend a one-hour meeting. Or get triple booked in back-to-backs on a Thursday. And yes, even work late into the night or all weekend long.

After a 20+ year career, one thing became clear to me. Hating the small stuff just gets in the way of loving the big stuff.

That's how I hope this book can help. To un-pain the pain points. To help push through the hateful stuff so you can feel the love once again. At least that's how I saw it, but it's not just me. Rather than filling these pages with my personal proclamations, I gathered opinions and insights from across the industry.

The first and most obvious question I asked everyone I spoke with was, "What do you hate about advertising?" I've kept the quotes anonymous because, you know, they might still like to have a career once this book comes out. Here's what they said:

"I really hate clients that are afraid."

"I hate data. There's less and less groundbreaking work these days. Everything is very efficient."

"Testing."

"Abrasive and sudden advertising that interrupts what I'm enjoying."

"It's not a fair business, never has been or will be."

"A lot of pointless meetings and pointless meetings about pointless meetings."

"I used to believe the best idea would win. It drives me crazy when that's not the case."

"Everyone has eyes and ears so apparently that means everyone has an opinion."

"At many big agencies it doesn't always feel like we are doing the 'solution thinking' part as much as we should be."

"I hate that so much of our fate can be out of our control. A client can at any moment, for some unforeseen reason, kill a campaign or idea you love. A pitch can go the other way for reasons you never saw coming or couldn't effect. But that's the cost of admission to a creative life that's also a business."

"Being made to feel like it will all be worth it in the end when in the end you're still making an ad to sell boxed mac and cheese to a mom while she's trying to watch some celebrity on Ellen or whatever."

"Your mark is never fully on what you leave behind as a creative."

"The constant, never-ending opportunity for disappointment."

"I hate working with people that don't like advertising."

"Sometimes, the industry gets in its own way."

"A lot of folks ask for swing for the fence (advertising), but they don't really mean it. So that's a waste of time and energy."

Then I asked, "What do you love about advertising?" I feel better about attributing names to these quotes.

"I love that something we thought of on the subway can be something everyone sees and is talking about across the world in a few weeks. I love that moment when you first come up with something that "solves it" and you can't wait to show others."
—Greg Hahn, Founder/CCO Mischief @ No Fixed Address

"I love how it's ever-changing. I love the people it collects and the doors it opens. Most of all, I love that if done right, it can affect culture in a really cool way."
—Samira Ansari, CCO (Ogilvy, Deutsch, FCB)

"I love the brilliant minds that I've come across over the years. The sheer intelligence, creativity and interesting ways that people see the world. I find that deeply moving. It's probably the thing that has kept me in the industry such a long time."
—Scott Goodson, CEO/Founder, StrawberryFrog

"Every single assignment, client, medium, and problem is truly unique and different. Nothing is repetitive. Nothing is boring."
—Sean Bryan, CCO (McCann, DDB, J. Walter Thompson [JWT])

"I love coming up with a commercial way more than the actual commercial."
—Rob Munk, CD/Writer (Arts & Letters, BBDO, W+K)

"I love that it's both creative and lucrative."
—Anjali Rao, CD/Writer (72andSunny, McKinney, Pereira O'Dell, FCB)

"We're gonna die (one day) and I think we have to leave something strong behind to inspire people. Advertising gives me that chance every single day."
—Pancho González, CCO/Founder Inbrax

"It's a constant challenge against yourself. You made a great idea, how can I beat myself the next time? That's what I love about the business."
—Camilo Ruano, CD/Art Director (Ogilvy, DDB, Pereira O'Dell)

"I love coming up with ideas. The more challenging it seems, the more you really think you are doing something new. I love that feeling. The drug is cracking the idea."
—Ivan Rivera, CD/Writer (Ogilvy, DDB, Pereira O'Dell)

"I love the invention. I love the idea that you're going to go do or say something new to solve a problem. That's what's really fun, coming up with those ideas."
—Grant Smith, CCO/Writer (Rise and Shine and partners, Yamamoto, McCann, BBDO)

"Well, it's better than a lot of other jobs. It's better than digging ditches or being an embalmer."
—Eric Stevens, CD/Art Director, Writer (Freelance, TBWA Chiat/Day, CAA, W+K)

"We get to play in the ether of humanity. And if it's done, well, we create idea viruses that will zing across the planet and back and that is intoxicating."
—Steve Conner, CEO, Fluid Content (Black GPT, HEPH Foundation, FCB, Burrell)

These last two responses covered both at the same time, in different ways:

"Love/Hate—that's honestly the best way to sum up advertising. Like most things in life, it swings between extremes. One minute, you're convinced you're a washed-up failure, wondering why you didn't start that pool cleaning business with your college buddy who's now somehow worth ten of your careers combined. The next minute? You're on the highest of highs, emotionally satisfied in a way no amount of clean pools could ever compete with. You get to see some weird, unexpected, deep-down part of yourself—maybe a part you didn't even know existed—come to life. You see this half-crazy idea that popped into your head at 2a.m., now on display for millions to experience. That's the magic. That's the love part. Taking something intangible, fleeting, fragile... and turning it into something real, impactful, and alive. A part of you out in the world, for the world to see."
—Josh DiMarcantonio, ECD/Writer (Zambezi, Deutsch, CAA, TBWA Chiat/Day, W+K)

"You have to figure out how to put your heart into something but not have your heart crushed by it."

—Alison Gragnano (The New School, Ogilvy, Saatchi&Saatchi, Margeotes Fertitta & Partners), ECD/Writer

Most people answered what they hate first, then the love. And the hate flowed a little easier than the love, which is why I'm writing this book. I hate that we have to address it all, but love getting the opportunity to work through it for myself, with everyone I talked to and with all you reading.

—Nick

Chapter 1

How not to hate advertising

"I hate advertising"

In 1982, the world of advertising changed forever with the meeting of two men, Phil Knight, the co-founder of Nike, and Dan Wieden, the co-founder of W+K. It went like this…"I'm Phil Knight and I hate advertising," said Phil, introducing himself to Dan just before Wieden pitched for the business. Dan replied, "Well, this is going to be interesting."[1] The rest is advertising history.

Seeing as Phil Knight, along with W+K, helped to invent much of what we love about advertising, he gets a pass. And when Knight said he hated advertising, he really meant most of the paid advertising in the world, which is garbage. It's true. He was right then. And he would be right today.

But this is not a "How To" create great advertising book. There are a lot of books about how to break into the business, how to write like a legend, or how to craft, kern, or code. The world doesn't need another one of those. This is a "How Not To" book.

What's a "How Not To" book, you ask? It's something you can turn to when you feel like you've had enough, or find yourself in a bind, want to avoid doing the wrong thing, or just want a reminder that there are thousands of other creatives out there, feeling the same things you're feeling. Something you can pick up to quiet your inner cynic, instead of falling into a deep morass of unhelpful self-loathing for a business that ain't that bad. A "How Not to" book is a little bit of mental jiu-jitsu, but just go with it. It's also a way better sales pitch. And that's the business we're in.

This is also not a book about ads themselves. I'm not here to say this campaign is great and that one is not. It's about the pain points of working as a creative (mostly) in the business. About how to fight off the things that might make you lose faith, get jaded, cynical, or want to quit doing the job. Or throw your laptop off a balcony. Or yell at your CD for not understanding your vision for the anthem song, which is way more relevant than whatever crap is in their Spotify wrapped.

DOI: 10.4324/9781032615707-1

This is for all of you who've felt the rage bubbling up inside like a can of Coke that if opened would unleash the opposite of a happiness factory.

Here's to the hateful ones.

The copywriters, the art directors, the designer and Design Directors, the Associate Creative Director (ACDs), CDs, SCDs, Group Creative Director (GCDs), ECDs, CCOs, EPs, Project Management (PM), Planners, and Account. The media buyers, the backend coders, and UXers. To the MDs who see things differently than you. To the Comms Strategists (Strat) who don't know why you don't understand programmatic. They are not always fond of advertising. But, yet they push the industry forward. And while they might see themselves as jaded or cynical, I still see hope. Because the people smart enough to recognize they might love this industry when they were starting out are the ones who can love it again.

Yes, even if your name is Clow, Droga, Goodby, Silverstein, Lubars, Hahn, Reilly, Graf, Hoffman, Rolfe, Credle, Kling, DeCourcy, Hegarty, Goodson, Pereira, Crispin, Porter, or Boguski, and you've enjoyed all the success in the world, you've probably said or felt like saying, "I hate advertising" at some point in your career. No? Well, congrats! This book probably isn't for you. Hope you saved your receipt. For everyone else, let's make a few things clear.

DON'T HATE IDEATE

Designer: Bryan Haker

First, an admission. I'm pretty confident I've never actually said the words, "I hate advertising" in my 23+ years in the business. If we ever worked together and you remember me saying it, I'll buy your copy of this book.

Something inside me won't let me say it, or think it. As hard as it gets, or as dumb or frustrating as it can seem, I don't hate it. And there's nothing else I really want to do, except maybe write movies and TV. But I can only imagine that's even more disappointing on a regular basis. Despite my eternal optimism, I've seen many people fall out of love, actively hate, lash out at, or try to distance themselves from the business, and I never really understood why. But maybe I'm the weirdo, because I knew I wanted to work in advertising in high school. MTV was the catalyst. The promos were like nothing I'd ever seen before. I was totally hooked. So, when I was offered my first full-time job in 2003 as a copywriter at MTV, I blurted out, "I'll take it!" before asking about salary, benefits, vacation days, etc. This was it. Requited love.

What was it like to work at MTV? Well, it was a looooong time ago. But it's probably what you imagine. I made Jimmy Fallon laugh. I was at a party with Jessica Simpson. I walked past Drew Barrymore after TRL and presented ideas for Beavis and Butt-Head's return to the VMAs. Mike Judge liked one of them enough to record it as Butt-Head. It said, "Call me Butt-Diddy." Ok, the Diddy part didn't age well, but to hear your joke come out of a character you loved as a kid was something I couldn't have ever imagined happening.

MTV was a great job, but not quite what I wanted. I didn't want to work on the same awards show year after year. I didn't want the same "clients" in marketing, whose office was just down the ball. Not in another city, state, or country. It was fun, but the stakes never felt that high. Sure, you could get away with fart jokes and celebrities were everywhere. Like when I was kinda sorta in the Foo Fighters for about 15 seconds, as they got ushered through a door to MTV Radio, and I got swept up among them. It was like a dream, but it wasn't my dream job. Agency life is what I really wanted.

I wanted the Madison Avenue experience I'd imagined. I wasn't getting advertising experience I thought shaped a career. New business pitches. Big-budget global TV shoots. Working across multiple brands. Winning over Chief Marketing Officers (CMOs). Presenting in a big room, with everything on the line. Climbing the creative ladder to CD, GCD, and beyond. Winning prestigious awards. Getting praise in industry pubs.

The ups and downs. The wins and losses. The accolades. The after-hours. The assholes. The free pizza in the conference room. The free wardrobe after the shoot. The chance to work at Wieden and write the next great "This is SportsCenter" spot. To win a gold pencil or be nominated for an Emmy. To have my work on the agency reel at a shop like BBDO. That's the advertising life I wanted. And that's the advertising life that created this book (Figure 1.1).

The chapters of this book were not picked at random. They contain real reasons people hate or lose faith in the business. Maybe even leave the business. Real things I had to navigate and overcome to ensure I didn't go down that path, because I've never wanted to leave. I still love advertising. And this book is sort of a recommitment to that love. A renewing of vows of sorts. Or maybe self-therapy? Whatever you want to call it, it's time to put it out there for anyone who needs a reminder.

Figure 1.1 Emmy nominated commercial "Childlike Imagination" for General Electric from BBDO. Courtesy of the Author.

Don't be a hater

Ok, now that I got all that uplifting, motivational speech stuff out of the way. Let's get real. Hate for an industry that you work in, that pays you really well, to come up with creative ideas that the world may actually see, and hopefully love (or at least, not hate), that you can do from home much of the time, that isn't manual labor and doesn't really start till 10 am? To say you hate that is pretty dumb, I think. So does Rob Munk (Arts & Letters, BBDO, W+K), CD/Writer, who says

> Feel incredibly lucky that you have a job that you have the luxury of disliking, you know. There are so many people that go to work and really hate what they do and have no choice. They have a much harder life. This is an easy, easy life. We all have soft hands.

I'm sitting in Dumbo House (part of SoHo House, a global members-only club) right now writing this, with my soft hands, a club that ridiculously enough wouldn't have accepted my membership if I didn't have a job from "the creative class." I have friends who work in finance who aren't able to join because of what they do for a living (and it drives them crazy). Yes, we have to put up with a lot coming up in this business, but let's not forget how great we got it. You can wear Crocs to work, for example. And you don't even have to be a doctor or a dishwasher to do it.

Ok, some less frivolous talk for a minute, as there are also some terrible sides to the industry that still need addressing. Diverse representation not just in the work we create, but those who create it is still a huge blind spot in the business. According to the Association of National Advertisers (ANA), Black talent in advertising only makes up 7.2% of the industry. The

4As found that "White-led ad agencies increased from 73% to 90% between 2021 and 2022." By their estimation, Black people made up even less of the share of talent than what ANA's metric suggested (6.99%).[2] The conversation isn't just black and white. It's multi-racial, gender, and ethnic, too. This unfair share of power and influence would be a totally fair reason to hate advertising and I wish this book had the answer, but it does not.

One reason for positivity lies in the gender makeup of the industry.

Female representation at the senior leadership level is 57.7% (according to the ANA board of directors and select member companies' diversity benchmark) and 59.9% in the analysis of the ANA member CMOs. Both are at the highest levels in the six-year history of the study.[3]

As an industry, we need to continue to look at ourselves in the mirror and ask what we can do to become more welcoming, accepting, and rewarding to the widest range of voices. There is a whole, hugely important conversation to be had and many books to be written on ways for the industry to become one we all collectively love. And loves us back.

Hate something. Change something

I would hate for anything that follows here to trivialize these harsh realities and long-overdue discussions. But, for what it's worth, this book is an exercise in helping you get through the more, let's call them annoying pain points in a creative's career. Like, what to do if you get shit from your boss for wearing a t-shirt to a new business pitch (this happened) or if it's okay to ignore your boss's text message at 11:30 pm (this also happened).

Maybe you have good reasons to hate advertising. Like, maybe you had to miss your niece's wedding for a presentation in Nashville that ended up being not at all worth it, and you parted ways with the client a year later. Or maybe you worked for two straight weeks on a huge pitch and stayed up till 5:30 am the night before the meeting, only to get one lousy print ad into the final deck. Or maybe you lost a pitch to a much safer agency or idea. And maybe you find out later that a client took your idea and gave it to another agency.

I hate it when that happens.

Or maybe you or your leadership wanted some competitive advantage so you pretended like you're not in the business you're in, and said, "We're not an ad agency. We hate ads!" Only to realize you mostly get briefed to create ads, and you work at an organization that would be best described as an agency. So you now hate that you made such a grand declaration, because you know, you work at an advertising agency.

All to say that if you have ever said, or felt like saying, those fateful words – "I hate advertising" – during your career, you've come to the right book.

A love/hate exercise

Let's use this section to try and remind yourself why you love this business in 100 words or less. Or use more than 100, I don't care. That's just the amount that will probably fit here. Also, you work in advertising, so saying it pithy and succinct is kind of your job. Go forth. Write it your way.

You didn't really write anything down, did you? Didn't think you would. You're a creative. You hate rules and corny exercises like that. I get it. If you *did* follow the assignment, how did it feel? Did it rekindle the flame? Remind you of why you fell in love in the first place? Or at least remind you that you used to like to draw or write with pen and paper?

Here are ten things that are more fun than advertising at any given time*

1   Shooting two feature-length films in one day
2   Going to a Boca Juniors match at La Bombonera
3   Writing lyrics for Snoop Dogg
4   Driving a MINI really fast
5   Writing jokes for Tina Fey
6   Skiing in waist high powder in Hokkaido, Japan
7   Playing in a Madden tournament on XBOX
8   Traveling to Scotland. Barcelona. Cape Town. Prague. Columbus, OH
9   Having Zach Wylde order a whiskey for you at the Sunset Marquis
10 Being awake on the old Las Vegas strip at 4:30 am with five Elvis imper-
    sonators and Roman Coppola

*Note: These are also things that were possible because of advertising, but would be objectively fun without it.

You are in the show business of business

When you think about it like this, it's hard to hate this job. You may hate how you don't go on as many production boondoggles as you used to and then sit in an edit for a month. Or hate that you don't get briefed on one big, Super Bowl TV ad and that's it. You may hate how you're sitting on Zoom all day and you have to put a hold on your calendar just to go to the bathroom or make a sandwich. You may hate your client's attitude. You may hate your account lead's lack of attitude. You may hate that your account lead is now your client. This is all totally understandable. But if you fixate on what you hate about what you do, a couple of things will happen:

1 You sound like a whiner, and nobody wants to work with a whiner. Even a whiner.
2 You begin to expect that your job should be perfect, which turns you into a whiner. See #1.

Cool story, bro. But what does it all mean? Here's the upshot, hot shot. I predict that by the end of this book, you'll either fall into one of two camps...

The Hater who realizes, "Yes, I do hate advertising. Thanks for confirming it! I'm gonna go sell all of my Jordans and go work at a fish market. 7-Up Yours suckas! I'm out!"

The I Got It Pretty Good-er who realizes,

You're right. We got it pretty, pretty, pretty good. Sure, the business is hard, but we get to think of ideas for a living, can afford $200 t-shirts and get put up at nice hotels while serving our creative compulsions that drive us and help us satisfy our career choices. Thanks for the reminder. I'm going to go write a Titanium winning social campaign for organic butter.

The next 40,000 words or so are here to help you figure out which one. But I didn't write them alone. Just like no campaign is created by one advertising executive wearing a full suit at 2 am drawing with their colored pencils like Hollywood would like you to believe. I needed help, insights, and wisdom from the many amazing contributors who so graciously gave me whatever time and wisdom they could (see the list of amazing people at the end of this section). The topics covered here aren't an exhaustive list. There's so much more to hate about advertising that didn't get covered, I'm sure. But that's what sequels are for! (Email my publisher and demand the follow-up now please, thanks.)

For all the non-creatives who picked up the book: Don't hate me. This was written from a creative standpoint because that's what I know, but I hope you find useful insights here as well. If not, well it wouldn't be the first time that a creative said a bunch of stuff you ignored. Maybe you can at least gain a little insight into why your creatives are such insecure pains in the asses all the time.

Ok, in the infamous last words of the convicted murderer Gary Gilmore in 1977[4], who inspired Dan Wieden to write the most famous tagline in advertising history:

Let's do it.

Here are the amazingly smart and talented people who generously agreed to participate in this book

Eric Stevens	CD, Art Director, Writer
Josh Dimarcantonio	ECD, Writer
Rob Munk	CD, Writer
Anjali Rao	CD, Writer
Camilo Ruano	CD, Art Director
Ivan Rivera	CD, Writer
Kurt Lenard	GCD, Art Director
Alan Buchanan	GCD, Art Director
Julie Rutigliano	ECD, Writer
Gary Van Dzura	ECD, Art Director
Ida Gronblom	ECD, Writer
Alison Gragnano	ECD, Writer
Jillian Goger	ECD, Writer
Scott Goodson	CEO/Founder, StrawberryFrog
Steve Conner	CEO/Founder, Fluid Content
Jeff Kling	CCO/Founder, Das Favorite
Greg Hahn	CCO/Founder, Mischief @ No fixed address
Pancho González	CCO/Founder, Inbrax
Ricardo Viramontes	CCO, Art Director
Samira Ansari	CCO, Art Director
Grant Smith	CCO, Writer
Sean Bryan	CCO, Writer
Rory Hill	Creative Recruiter/Talent Director
Lisa Preston	VP of Marketing
Jim Lee	Artist/Professor of Fine Arts, Design, Art History

Notes

1 "Nike co-founder Phil Knight remembers Dan Wieden." Phil Knight. Campaign Asia. October 7, 2022.
2 "Black talent remains underrepresented in advertising industry." hrdive.com Caroline Colvin February 23, 2024.
3 "ANA report shows ethnic diversity among marketers declining." February 15, 2024.
4 "Just do it! How murderer Gary Gilmore's final words demanding firing squad officers pull their triggers inspired Nike's famous slogan." Harry Howard. Dailymail.co.uk, January 17, 2022.

Chapter 2

How not to hate the creative process

The creative process is just about the most anxiety-inducing and delightfully painful part of the business. Whether that's your personal process, or the universal process to go from a blank page to closing the job number. It can and should be painful, excruciatingly at times. You aren't curing cancer (unless you're in pharma), but you are solving a crucial business problem. That could be trying to convince someone from Oklahoma with only a couple of teeth left to buy an electric toothbrush. Or trying to sell a small electric car in a country obsessed with gas-guzzling trucks. Or trying to get people to get excited about a restaurant that isn't opened yet in a building that isn't built yet. These are hard problems to solve creatively. I've had to solve all of these and they all came with plenty of pain. As I like to say about poker, which I used to play often with other creatives and agency types, I've never won without feeling really uncomfortable. When you know you have a great hand, the pressure is on, the stakes are high, and you are walking a tightrope not to screw it up. How many presentations have felt like that? Actually, don't tell me.

Not every advertising problem is difficult, but the creative process always will be. It can also be cathartic and invigorating. Like when you crack a campaign line for that electronic toothbrush for the dentally challenged, "Cele-bright clean teeth, come on!" DO NOT STEAL THAT. YOU'LL GET FIRED.

So why shouldn't you hate the creative process?

Honestly, you probably should. And you definitely will at times. But look at it this way: if creativity was easy, you wouldn't want to do it. When did you stop coloring in coloring books? When it got too easy, or you got too old. If anyone could paint like Van Gogh, we wouldn't be in awe of *Starry Night*. We do this job not just because we know how to, but because we take pleasure in knowing not everyone can. There, I said it. Creatives are ego-driven narcissists who think they're better than everyone else. To some degree, we are. All of us. But because the creative process is so difficult, you have to be.

DOI: 10.4324/9781032615707-2

The creative process is like getting repeatedly punched in the face and continuing to wake up and do it again. Say you get punched in the face ten times. It hurts every time. But if you're still standing after the eleventh? Smiling even? Well, then you're creative. And a badass. You're probably also delirious, but that means "in a state of wild excitement or ecstasy." So, you got that going for you.

Ida Gronblom (Anomaly, FCB, 72andSunny, W+K) is a super-talented ECD. She equates the creative process to another painful and life-altering experience, as the mother of two children.

"I really love being pregnant with an idea, and then (you get) that rush of adrenaline when it's birthed and put out in the world. You forget about the pain that came with it and then you go at it all over again. That's how women have more children, because they forget how painful it is."

Creativity is unlike any other type of pain because you don't want to avoid it. A presentation won't feel right without it. If you arrive at an idea much too easily, that's a whole other kind of pain. The embarrassing kind, not the creatively fulfilling kind. The creative pain only hurts for a little while but it leads to something great. The embarrassing kind leads to an unimpressed client and a rambling post-mortem in which everyone is deflated and lost. Nothing that's any good is easy and nothing that's easy is any good. If you're not uncomfortable at some point in the process, you're doing it wrong.

Figure 2.1 Ida Gronblom. ECD, Writer.

Ida added to this point when she said, "I end up with mediocre work when I trick myself into feeling like I have (a great idea), because I just want it to be over and I just want something to be bought. You shouldn't do that."

No pain no gain, right? Wrong. No pain, you skipped a step. This isn't about becoming a creative martyr or telling yourself to "trust the process." It's about wrapping your arms around the process and giving it a big, old sweaty bear hug. But what parts of the process am I talking about? Remember those ten punches to the face? They may come in the form of...

1 The brief
2 Creative reviews
3 Feedback
4 The internal
5 More feedback!
6 The 11th-hour bomb
7 Starting over
8 Even more feedback!
9 Working late
10 Craft

To be clear this chapter doesn't pretend to have all the answers to help you master the creative process so that you become the most highly-awarded and sought-after creative in the world. If I knew that, this book would cost roughly 23 Bitcoin. Or I would've paid someone to ghostwrite it for me. No. This chapter will address some key pain points of the creative process in hopes of helping you hate them a little less. Or at least, soften the blow.

How not to hate: the brief

Note this section says the brief, not the briefing. No one hates a briefing. At least, no creatives I know. The briefing is the best. That's when a project is filled with endless possibilities. When the project seems inspiring and important. Visions of Lions dance in your head. You're on the cover of *AdAge*. SNL is spoofing your idea. SMASH CUT to an hour or two later, and you're now holding the one-page brief and that's when it hits you, "WTF am I supposed to do with this?" That brief that used to be filled with opportunity is now staring at you, judging you, taunting you, laughing at you. You hate everything about it. The insight. The background. The stupid font it's written in. You wonder, *Can't we just come up with something cool and make strategy back rationalize it?* Maybe, if you're lucky. But for most of us, that's a medium-to-hard no. Clients have invested way too much time and money in this piece of paper. It's how they hold the agency accountable (until *they* change it) and how the agency will know if they're doing it right, or just trying to be creative. Nothing wrong with either of those things, btw.

Relax. Breathe. It's not the brief's fault. And even if it is, you're way past that. The briefing happened. The schedule was shared. Creative reviews and internals are on your calendar. You need to make something happen. Anything.

Ok, so where's the "not hate it" part? Well, here it is.

That brief you hate is about to save your life. Not because it's going to help you *come up* with the idea. It's going to save your life because it has all the information you need to *sell* your idea. That's right. The brief may be written to inspire ideation. But once you get there, it becomes a valuable tool. No, a weapon. It's time to use it for all it's worth. Sell it back to the client. After all, they agreed that's what this idea should be about. It's all right there.

Imagine the brief said, "Our new line of smart appliances alert you before they break down, so they never interrupt the special moments at home, which leads to a happier and healthier life for you and your family." You could certainly justify presenting a five-part content series about a family named The Smarts who live in perfect harmony with their talking refrigerator, oven, and dishwasher, who have all become members of the family like Alf meets Knight Rider meets the Jetsons. When your client looks at you like you're from outer space, could just point back to the brief.

Or the brief said, "We want companies to see New York State as a place to start and grow their business." So, you present the idea of converting unused office buildings into spaces for entrepreneurs to get their businesses off the ground, free of rent for a year. Your idea is to advertise those places that actually give businesses a place to start and grow, instead of just an ad campaign telling people to come to New York. And when your client says, "But we wanted a TV commercial that said business is better in NY." You could point to the brief and say, "Actually, you said you wanted to bring businesses to New York and with this idea, you can."

Before you can even get to the point of wielding the brief like a weapon, first you need a great idea. Those ideas don't just have to pop into your brilliant mind. They need to be written down, presented, and survive the first hurdle in the process you might hate if it doesn't go well.

How not to hate: creative reviews

Let's pretend for a second you just picked up this book because it had an intriguing title but you don't work in an agency or know anything about how they work. The creative review (CR) is the first checkpoint after getting briefed, where you now get to tell someone – other than your partner, your spouse, or your golden retriever – all the amazing ideas you came up with to answer the brief. Who are you telling these ideas to? One of the following CDs above you.

ACD:	Associate Creative Director
CD:	Creative Director
SCD:	Senior Creative Director
GCD:	Group Creative Director
ECD:	Executive Creative Director
CCO:	Chief Creative Officer

CSGSVPCD: Chief Senior Global Executive, SVP Creative Director (this title does not exist, but it definitely could).

You get the idea.

Depending on which side of the idea sharing you're on during a CR – bringing the ideas or shaping the ideas – things will look different. So let's break it up appropriately.

How not to hate a CR, if you're a creative

Creative reviews aren't just meetings. They're like an open mic with an audience of one or two overbooked CDs. There's never enough time to prepare. Never enough ideas in your deck. Never enough of a reaction from your CD. Meanwhile, you're feeling any or all of the following: Anxiety. Fear. Elation. Disappointment. Sadness. Joy. Anger. Jealousy. Resentment. Swagger. You feel good. You feel bad. You feel like a genius. You feel like a hack. And that's just while going through the first idea or two.

Feeling the hate? Get over it, because this is actually the best part of the process. You get to talk about ideas in hopes that one of them eventually gets made. Do whatever you have to do to get your head straight before the review. Scream into a pillow. Take a shot of whiskey. Play Wordle while listening to Slayer. *And remember this,* your CD wants to like your ideas. It may not always feel that way, but you having great ideas means their life just got easier. If you figure it out, they won't have to. Even if you haven't figured it all out, that's fine. That's the reason for the review.

Keep the hate in check by keeping these things in mind...

- Remember, your ideas are just the beginning of a conversation.
- Know that the goal of the first CR is to see if there are any paths worth going down. Almost nothing will survive, but it should lead to a better idea.
- The second CR is for the refinement of your first ideas and to review new ideas. Don't forget the new ideas, unless you truly want to hate the experience.
- A CR could become a concepting session for your CD. They haven't thought about it since the briefing and need to play catch up.
- No reaction doesn't mean your CD hates an idea. They're trying to figure out how to improve it or sell it.
- If you're lucky enough to have PM taking notes in your CR, it means you can stay in the moment with the idea.
- If your CD gives you an idea in a CR, get over the fact that it wasn't yours. Take it and make it great.
- If your CD hates all of your ideas, relax. It doesn't mean they hate you.
- Bring the brief. Your CD will need a reminder.

How not to hate a CR, if you're a CD

What appears to be just another meeting on your triple-booked calendar can quickly become the best part of your day. This is especially true if the ideas are great, and sometimes even if not. This is why you got into the business, and what keeps you in it – IDEAS. Wild ideas. Smart ideas. Crazy ideas. Stupid ideas. Can we do this legally ideas. If you're lucky, you'll find yourself having the most ridiculous conversations you have all day/week/year in a CR. It's a safe space, filled with unsafe ideas. Greg Hahn (CCO/Founder of Mischief @ No Fixed Address USA) said it best, "I love that we spend our days discussing, 'Is that something a merman would say?'" We are all Merman linguists, just remember that.

Figure 2.2 Greg Hahn. CCO/Founder, Mischief @ No fixed address.

A CR is our TV show writer's room. Our SNL pitch day. Our Warhol's Factory. It's only a shame that we don't have more time to spend on them. If creatives ran the process, we'd have four or five reviews before bringing in the wider team. We'd spend weeks dreaming up the impossible. But at some point, you have to step out of the sandbox and show people the castles you've been building. But before you do, give the creatives your full attention, manage your expectations, and keep the following in mind:

- Don't expect greatness. Expect bits of greatness. It's your job to piece them together.
- Don't give the creatives the answer. Give them a problem to solve. A kernal to pop.
- Don't expect the solution to be how you would solve it. You want ideas you couldn't have come up with.
- Everything you say could be taken as feedback. Make sure creatives know what is and isn't.
- Don't close more doors than you open.
- Don't forget to ask for the brief. Good creatives will have it handy.

How not to hate a CR, if you're anyone else

If you're not a creative and you get invited to a CR, you're there to observe, ask questions, or identify ways to support the ideas. You're not there to judge or approve them. That's the easiest way to get disinvited to future

CRs. You were invited because time was tight, or you have some insight the CD doesn't, or there's an idea that needs a tricky setup. This is a creative's safe space, tread carefully.

How not to hate: feedback

If you've ever had management training, giving productive feedback would've been one of the key lessons. Forget all that. This is about creative feedback, on creative ideas, to creatives. Those insecure, vulnerable, sensitive, artsy people with chips on their shoulders the size of One Show pencils. And therapy bills longer than Arnell's 2004 Pepsi rebrand deck. Creative feedback exists for one reason: to help develop an idea further. It's not personal. It's not profound. It's instructional and ideally inspiring. It should tell you what's not working, not how to fix it.

DON'T HATE THE FEEDBACKER HATE THE FEEDBACK

Designer: Bryan Haker

How not to hate getting feedback, if you're a creative

The reality is, there's no way to not hate getting feedback as a creative, even if it's just a tiny bit. You can deal with it your own way, but getting it always stings. Not the easy notes, like *Can you show us a few other font choices?* But on the bigger stuff, like "We like the idea, just not the story, the voiceover, the characters, the ending or the tagline." That's never easy. If you can keep your mouth shut long enough to let them say whatever they have to say, you'll be better off. Stay quiet. Stay stoic. Don't solve it in the moment. Hear them out. Whoever they are.

Figure 2.3 Jillian Goger. ECD, Writer.

Jillian Goger (Mekanism, Droga5, McCann, Arnold), a veteran freelance ECD/writer, has a rule about feedback, but it's not exactly hard and fast. "I used to coach my creative teams not to respond to any client comments until the decision maker weighed in. And then I'd inevitably break my own rule in frustration with the baby brand manager who went first."

See? It's hard. This is your work. You want to defend it, explain it, and not change it. But the reality is, it's your idea, but someone else is paying for it. So it's going to change. To what degree depends on how you control the hate.

How not to hate giving feedback, if you're a creative leader

Stop saying "Here's what I would do." It's deflating to creatives and makes it all about you. They will write down how you said you would do it, and just do that. They'll also be guessing what you want and it'll shut down their ability to solve the problem creatively. It may *seem* like a nice way of imparting some wisdom. I'm sure it feels instructional and inspiring. Best of intentions, I get it. But it doesn't work. You're better off saying, "There's something really exciting about this idea. Where else can you take it?" This puts it back on them to solve the issue. They'll leave excited about the potential, not stymied by prescriptive direction.

If you really do want them to execute it your way, give them a specific example. Or, better yet, do it yourself. But remember, isn't about you. So don't do that. Unless they are really struggling and it's time to step in and save the day. But that's not feedback. That's just being a boss.

Rule #1: avoid the vague like the plague

Stop trying to make all the decisions in the creative review. If you don't have the right words, follow up. You're better off sending them back to the well than confusing them with fragmented half-thoughts. But a simple "Keep going" isn't helpful either. Tell them *why* the idea isn't working. It's okay to hate everything, but you should say why and then give them a place to start. A nugget that's working, a word with potential, a reference that's exciting, so they know how to start again.

Rule #2: there's no reason to be harsh

Advertising used to be a business where being harsh was a badge of honor. For some, becoming a CD meant needing to show everyone just how passionate you were about the work. If you didn't rip ideas off the wall, or kill an entire round, or yell at someone for bringing you garbage, you were doing it wrong.

That just doesn't fly anymore. This business is hard enough. Assholes need not apply. Being hard on the work is fine. Being hard on people is not. Creatives will feel your passion by the ideas you get excited about, not the ones you rail against. Save this rage for the gym, bro (more on that in Chapter 11).

Rule #3: see rules #1 and #2

There's a thing called "The rule of 3s" and who am I to defy it?

How not to hate sharing feedback – if you're in Strat, Account, or PM

Realize it's going to take a while for the feedback to resonate. Creatives are a sensitive bunch, but you know that already. They don't all have the ability to see what's behind the notes. They see it all as an attack on their idea (and/or ego). Be selective, weed out the notes that aren't actionable, or risk the swirl if you don't. Don't just take the client notes and email them. Sift through, pick out the important things. Rewrite them for creative minds, if you have time. Set up a meeting, even if you don't have time – you'll save time in the end, by making sure it's clear. Feedback is a delicate moment in the process. It can really help. It can also seriously derail, so handle with care.

How not to hate giving feedback, if you're a client

As a client, your job is remarkably easy. If you abide by this one rule, your agency partner will love working with you. Tell the agency *why* something isn't working, *not how* to fix it. That's it. Simple. Oh, always start with something like, "Thank you for all of the amazing ideas. We really enjoyed them…" You can say almost anything after that and it will be received well. Except for maybe, "you're fired." Or "It's a total redo."

How not to hate getting truly terrible feedback from a client

Smile. Nod. Stall. Say "Let us have a think about that" or "I'm gonna write that one down and get back to you," then take a deep breath. Then, ask them questions, like "What's not working for you about the cat's fur color?" and "Is your biggest issue with our hero talent the size of his earlobes?" Or "I understand your boss doesn't like the color green, is there another color that won't make him puke?" Be nice about it, but not too nice. They'll sniff out your sarcasm pretty quick. Truly terrible client feedback is actually kind of amazing. Seriously, write it all down. You'll want to look back on it one day, or you know, maybe write a book about it.

Fun fact: The BEST piece of feedback I ever received was at MTV. My partner Thomas Berger and I were assigned a print ad to congratulate Ozzy Osbourne on his 25 years in the music business, so we created an illustrated ad of the dove head he bit off on stage, to do the congratulating. The only feedback we got? "Can you add more blood?" Yes, yes we can. And did (Figure 2.2).

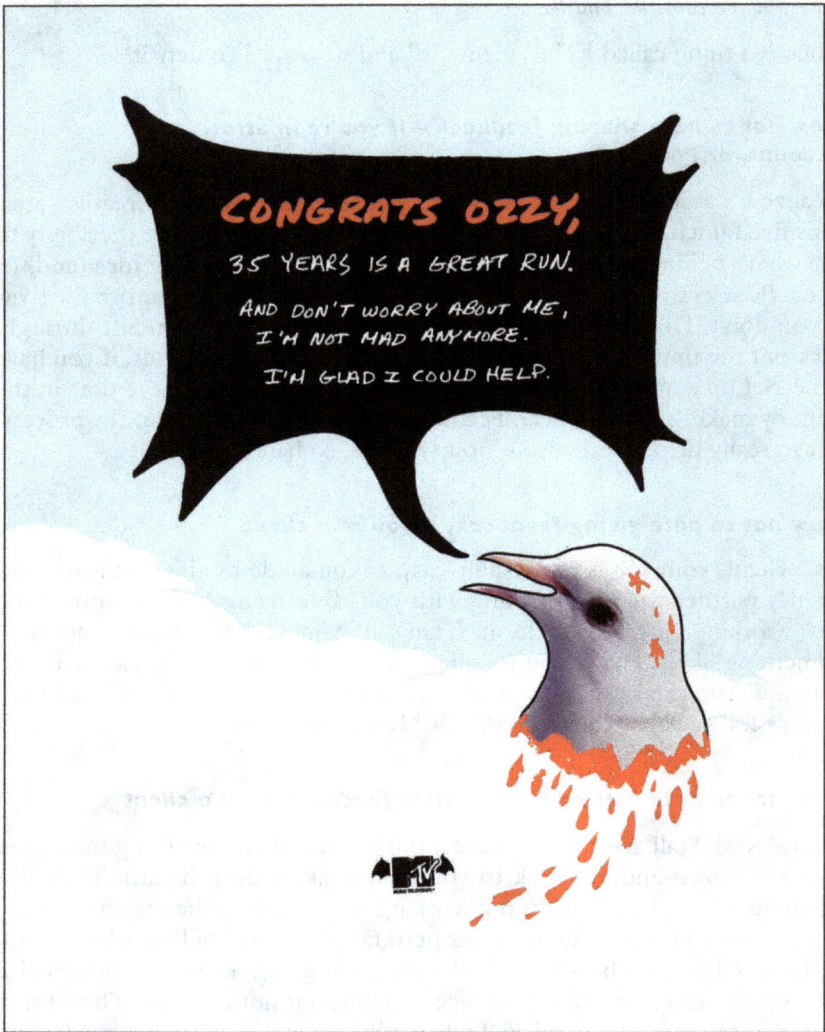

Figure 2.4 "Add more blood." Best feedback ever on this Ozzy Osbourne Congrats ad for MTV. Provided by the author.

How not to hate: the internal

Ah, the internal. Everyone's favorite meeting, except the creatives. You've been working away, and now is the time to show everyone what you got. And defend your ideas from dying before they even get to the client. Believe it or not, this is part of the creative process. Putting the idea down on paper is step one. Putting the idea out there to see if it's any good is the next step.

If you were a painter, this would be like a soft opening of your new exhibit. You'd invite friends and family and give them a preview before the public sees it. But you are not a painter (professionally) and this isn't exactly the right analogy because imagine a painter going through what we go through. They spend days creating a series of paintings, only to then share them with a select few people for their opinions, who then expect their comments to be addressed in the work before the public viewing. Let's not imagine. Let's ask an actual artist and tenured Professor of Fine Arts at Hofstra University, Jim Lee, what he thinks.

> The gallery makes studio visits to check on progress, other artists make studio visits and offer criticism and/or advice…whether asked for or not. I like to say, hear everything that is being said, but only listen to what applies to my intentions.

Imagine having that luxury in advertising. Jim then went on to quote someone who definitely didn't have to listen to anyone but himself, Pablo Picasso. "When art critics get together they talk about Form and Structure and Meaning. When artists get together they talk about where you can buy cheap turpentine." So, basically – take your opinion and shove it.

But I repeat, this isn't art. This is advertising. And you can't avoid the internal. So what's the "how not to hate" lesson for this part of the process? It's actually quite simple: Just because people make comments at the internal, doesn't mean you have to change anything if you don't want to. You should listen, be respectful, and say things like "Good point," or "That's interesting," or "I hadn't thought about that" and then…it's okay to do nothing, or only change it if you really want to. Depending on the agency dynamics, naturally. And depending on whether someone in the internal does in fact have a good point worth addressing.

But the reality is, the internal isn't designed to be a meeting where everyone gets to have a say on the work. Done right, it's a gut check to make sure you (and they) don't look like total idiots in the client presentation.

Creatives are still the ultimate arbiters of an idea. This is a painful reality for some in the room. But if creative is the product we're selling in our business, then creative gets the final say on what goes to the client. Simple as that.

How not to hate: More feedback!

Ugh. Take a long walk. Then see point #3.

How not to hate: the eleventh-hour CCO/ECD/GCD bomb

You *think* you thought of everything. You've gone through the whole grueling process, gotten comments and buy-in from internal teams, and are putting a final coat of paint on the best-looking rocket ship you've ever created. Blast off is tomorrow at 10 am with clients. Then, your CCO/ECD/GCD asks how the work is coming along. "Shoot it over to me," they say. And that's when it happens…BOOM. An eleventh-hour bomb goes off. You can freak out or you can be prepared, knowing it might happen. I once briefed creatives at 9:30 pm the night before a 10 am presentation in Chicago (in person!), and was reviewing new scripts at 1:30 am to decide what gets in – all because my CCO wanted new ideas. It's okay to freak out a little, but it won't help you in the end.

What can you do?

Mentally prepare. Know a bomb like this might be coming. This kind of eases the pain. Prep your flak jacket and canteen.

Save an idea or two for this very moment. Those half-thoughts come in handy. You could even pre-brief a team/writer on ideas, knowing a bomb might go off. Fill your arsenal with a few secret weapons.

Take whatever idea the CCO/ECD/GCD offers up and run with it. It's late. They want to have a say. Make it work. It doesn't mean it will sell, but you look good.

How not to hate: starting over

Figure 2.5 Alison Gragnano. ECD, Writer.

"Once a client put us on mute only they didn't actually put us on mute, and we heard them trying to explain how they were going to tell us that they were going to pretty much kill everything." This is a brutal story from Alison Gragnano (The New School, Ogilvy, Saatchi&Saatchi, Margeotes Fertitta & Partners), Executive Creative Director/Writer, but all too common, save for the "on mute" mistake.

There's no easy answer to how not to hate starting over. You just have to get used to it. Make that transition in your mind, from hanging onto your ideas like your firstborn to killing your darlings. The day you realize there's always another great idea is the day you make this part a little easier. You will need a break. Work in a different room from before. Go to a different coffee shop.

Open a new notebook, or grab a new pen. Enter a restart as fresh as possible.

Creatives have to do this so many times, it becomes second nature. But don't get me wrong, it's never easy. You can be Zen about it. Or you can do what Gary Van Dzura (BBH, W+K, R/GA) does.

> I like to craft a new argument while I'm pissed. 'Oh, that idea doesn't work? Then what about this?!' After you get that out, then the next day you can start over with (something) new. You can't pout about it.

Or maybe you can? Because sometimes, the idea isn't really dead. This has happened to Gary and may happen to you, too.

Figure 2.6 Gary Van Dzura. ECD, Art Director.

> Some things are never dead. They can always come back. Ideas in a presentation might come back two, three years later, and then all of a sudden, you're making a thing that you thought was completely gone, because the clients might have liked it, but maybe the time wasn't right. So, you never know and never give up on it.

Looking for a reason not to hate the idea dying and having to start over? That's a great one.

Another approach is to always be starting over, as Pancho Gonzalez, CCO/Founder at Inbrax does.

> I don't fall in love with what I did in the past. That could be

Figure 2.7 Pancho González. CCO/ Founder, Inbrax.

something that I did yesterday or last week. If it's done, I forget that and (think) what's next? As a mindset, a daily mindset, every single day, I start with a white page. I'm like an intern every single day of my life. So I think that you know, having that (mindset) will really help you to not hate advertising.

How not to hate: Even more feedback!

You've got to be kidding me…

How not to hate: working late

Let's face it. Working late is not fun. See above 9:30 pm briefing story. You'd rather be doing just about anything else than trying to crack a new platform for a pasta brand at 10:15 pm or writing a manifesto for a QSR until 1:28 am. That said, cranking into the wee hours is like feedback or testing, you can hate it, but it ain't going nowhere. There was a time I didn't hate working late when I was but a humble, mid-level copywriter. Why? Two words. Dinner stipend.

It's amazing the power $20 has on a young, broke writer's motivation. For creatives of today who are probably putting in late nights at home in your pajamas, it used to be if you were at the agency past, say 8 pm, you could expense dinner up to a certain amount. And when I discovered that a six-pack of beer was roughly the same amount as a sandwich from a NYC bodega, and finance accepted a non-itemized receipt from my local deli…let's just say I didn't mind staying late. Also, odds are that you weren't the only one working late, so there was always pizza somewhere in the agency. This meant you could eat free pizza, then also expense "dinner" for $20. Times have changed, so how can you curb your hate for working late?

Here's an incomplete list of ideas:

If you know a late night is inevitable, go do something else first. Go to the gym, or a movie in the middle of the day, or that thing at your kid's school at 1:15 pm. You'll regret missing that more than the extra hours on a brief that night.

Keep track of all the late hours, and demand comp time. Management won't say no.

Switch out of your work sweatpants into your house sweatpants. This change is stupidly helpful.

Work hard for one hour, then take a 15-minute break. Then another hour, then another 15-minute break. And so on, and so on.

Pick a time to finish. It's less daunting if you know there's an end.

Have one beer, or one glass of wine, or one microdose to make the late-night hours more tolerable. But any more than one and you're not really working anymore.

How not to hate: craft

"Craft, schmraft. If it doesn't have heart, who gives a shit?" – Alan Buchanan (Apple, Wieden+Kennedy New York [WKNY]), GCD/AD.

I see Alan's point, but also don't totally believe him. When Alan and I worked together at WKNY, he stayed later than any other AD in the agency. Always tweaking and crafting. Yes, creatives are big idea people. But we are also small details people. If you're not given the time you need to craft, that's one thing. If you do have it and don't take it, that's a missed opportunity. The Lions are in the details. Hone the hell out of everything within your reach – from a headline to the layout, to the case study, and to the PR angle for the press release. Everything surrounding an idea is a creative's responsibility to craft. If you don't, you will hate yourself for not caring more once it's done and out in the world. But to Alan's point, first make sure it's got enough heart to be worth it.

At the end of the day, a great idea is worth the wait

Creativity is a math equation with infinite inputs and outcomes. Or maybe more of a science experiment. As you plug in all of the inputs, variables, and outside stimuli, it always comes down to one thing: *TIME*. You'll never have enough, and the clients will demand more with less. But inasmuch as it is within your control, you should always take the time you need. Account can wait. Production can wait. Clients can wait. Deadlines can shift. Spots can be reshipped.

Kerning, deck flow, a period after a tagline – these things matter. Even at a time when "good enough" is becoming the standard, creatives must remember the fine line between craft and crap. Fight the fights, but only the good ones (aka, the fight worth winning).

Jim Collins popularized the phrase, "Good is the enemy of great" in his book *Good to Great: Why Some Companies Make the Leap...and Others Don't*.[1] In advertising, that can mean the difference between a shortlist and a bronze. Winning or losing a pitch. It's like the classic Nike headline that remains a favorite of mine. "You don't win silver, you lose gold." That could've just as easily been a philosophy about craft in advertising, as it was about being an Olympic athlete.

The current atmosphere of insane deadlines, demanding clients, and faster tools (i.e., AI) can affect the attention to detail that craft requires, to take work to the next level. So that you (and everyone else) don't hate what you put out into the world. And that's all we're trying to do here, right? Love, not hate, the things we create.

Note

1 *Good to Great: Why Some Companies Make the Leap...and Others Don't.* Jim Collins. Harper-Collins Publishers, 2001.

Chapter 3

How not to hate your own brand

There's a brand out there that you know better than any, that only you are qualified to work on. It's more valuable than Coca-Cola or McDonald's, more high maintenance than Anheuser-Busch or Samsung, and could make you as famous as Nike or Adidas. Yet, it's a brand that can't be pitched and won because that brand is *you*.

It won't be easy. Believe me. Yours is the hardest brand to sell, especially for a creative. Why? Are you too close to it? Well, yeah. Does it have so many great qualities that it's hard to prioritize? Uh huh. Is it a clearly defined brand like Apple or Nike? Well, that's the problem. So, let's figure it out.

Brand you, not brand new

It used to be that your work alone could sell you to anyone. That's still mostly true, but there are so many other ways today to demonstrate your creative prowess. Obviously, having a great portfolio is key (Chapter 6), but so are awards (Chapter 10), being fluent in new technologies, like AI (Chapter 9), having a creative side project (Chapter 6), and mastering the art of self-promotion (this chapter).

Why are we so good at selling brands and so bad at selling our own? Are we too brain-dead from putting all of our energy into client work? Maybe. Or is it that we can't hide behind a product feature, or a brand manifesto? Or does it just feel gross to talk about yourself? Probably. Is that why so many creatives write about themselves on their site in the third person? According to Rory Hill (By Royal Appointment, Pereira O'Dell, 72and-Sunny, W+K), Recruiter and Talent Director, you may want to stop doing that. "It's okay if you want to write in the third person, but don't make a joke about it, because that joke is very old."

DOI: 10.4324/9781032615707-3

Figure 3.1 Rory Hill. Recruiter, Talent Director.

Ok, so maybe the cleverness you thought would set you apart by writing about yourself in the third person *wasn't* so unique. Good thing you're reading this chapter, which should hopefully give you some new ways of thinking about your own brand. Or at least, how not to hate selling yourself. First, you have to figure out your brand voice. And it's fairly easy if you just do what you already do for clients.

1   **Brief yourself**
2   **Define your voice**
3   **Sell, baby, sell**

Only this time, you have to play every role – the Strat, writer, art director, CD, and agency founder, who could come in and blow up the whole project at any point. But whatever. You're also the client. So, you get the final sign-off.

Brief yourself

First of all, just to be clear. You don't have to actually *do* any of the following. This isn't an actual assignment. You are not an actual brand. So, put pen to paper (or keyboard to cloud doc), if you want, but obviously don't have to if that feels too weird. What you *do* need to do though is think about it. Really carefully. What do you want people to remember about your brand? If you don't do it yourself, the talent leads and CDs at agencies will do it for you. They will define you in ways you may or may not want, by talking about you like this…

"He's a comedy guy"
"She's an edgy, street art type"
"They are an 'epic anthems' team"
"She only does emotional work"
"They're mostly social"
"He's an innovation guy. He might actually be AI"
"He's a writer's writer"

"They are the activations team."
"He's good for hard accounts."
"They're a Super Bowl team"

And so on.

These are all fine and good ways to be described. You can make a career on any number of the above descriptions. All I'm saying is, don't let them put baby in a corner unless that's the corner you want to put it, baby. Sorry for calling you baby. Don't cancel me.

Some years ago, I was in LA during shoot prep when someone on the production side asked what I did at the agency. I said, "I'm a writer." I didn't say "I'm a Creative Director" or "I'm in charge of leading this campaign and brand." I said, "writer." I can't say why because I don't know why. It just came out. When I think back on it, I probably said it because it was the simplest explanation. People know what a writer is, and isn't that our job as advertisers? To boil something complicated down into a simple, digestible message? Sure. But our job is also to be creative, interesting, and memorable. I'm not sure how memorable the one-sentence tagline for brand me would be...

Nick Sonderup, Writer

...but it would been clear. And sometimes clarity over cleverness is the best way forward. Like at our day jobs, it all depends on the audience. For the sake of this chapter, your audience is people in and around the advertising industry.

And since we don't do anything without a brief, below is a brief for you to get started. You probably won't actually do it, but at least read it. And think about it. When is the presentation? That's up to you.

Brand: You

Agency: You

The Assignment: What are you trying to accomplish?

Identify a meaningful brand positioning for (your name) that genuinely connects in an authentic and memorable way with recruiters and senior creative leaders by creating differentiation in today's saturated creative professional landscape.

The enemy: What are you pushing against?

Conformity. Dullness. Forgettability.

How will you measure success?

The ultimate measure of success depends on your KPIs, but some suggestions follow. (1) Not having your LinkedIn requests or messages ignored. (2) Having your emails returned and work reviewed. (3) Getting hired for a project or job. (4) Having clients or former colleagues describe you the same way you describe yourself on LinkedIn or by word of mouth.

Who is the target?

Senior talent, creative leaders, recruiters, hiring, and talent managers. CMOs, CEOs, senior clients, awards show judges, and industry press.

What's the key message?

See next section...

Define your voice

"Find your unique voice. And make sure it's true to you. Nobody can compete with you at being you." – Greg Hahn, CCO/Founder of Mischief @ No Fixed Address USA.

Defining your voice is as crucial as it is for the brand you're working on. And you can do all the same things you do for your clients. Like, write a manifesto and tagline for "brand (your name)" or hone your own personal new business narrative. But let's be honest. No one's going to do any of those things, and that's fine.

Your work is the strongest way to bring that voice to life. The more you put yourself into the idea, the more people will see it. An old partner of mine from WKNY, Alan Buchanan, who now works at Apple, has a very specific style of humor and sensibility. He's not even a "comedy guy" but I know right away when I see an Apple spot that Alan has touched. It could be an expression, it could be a song choice, or a simple line of dialogue – but when I see it, I know it was Alan. The same goes for another former friend and partner from my WKNY days, Gary Van Dzura. Once I saw a Fox Sports spot with Mariah Carey in it and immediately thought, "How did Gary book her?" I texted him and he told me the story.

Your work helps define your voice, but it's not the only step. How you present the work and yourself is where you can dial things up or down, to find the perfect pitch.

Do you want to be a bottle rocket or a strike anywhere match

It's an age-old question for creatives in advertising: Should you specialize or generalize? Do you want to be the one creating the next NBA campaign? Or creating a campaign for a brand advertising during the NBA season? The answer is: yes. And both. Is there an actual right answer to this question? As one of Barack Obama's most famously meme-d speeches says, with infinite hilarity, "Not really. Maybe? It's classified." The real answer is it depends on you, where you are in the career, and where you want to take it. Personally, it's helped me to be more of a multi-tool. Specializing can be great because people know when to call you. But it can also put you in a box, and keep some from texting for your avails.

How not to hate being an advertising multi-tool

You'll get a lot more briefs because people will think you can crack anything, not just the funny thing or the emotional thing. Plus, you could call yourself Leatherman and that sounds pretty rad. Most of us start out as a Leatherman (Leather-woman, or Leather-they), according to Rory Hill (By Royal Appointment, Pereira O'Dell, 72andSunny, W+K). "At the start of your career, you're encouraged to do everything, partly to survive, and partly because you're still learning. (Then) there's a point, when you're a senior, you're going to be faced with a quandary." That quandary is what to specialize in, or whether to specialize at all. If you specialize, should that be in comedy? Emotion? Activations? Digital? Social? Entertainment? AI? Pharma? Multicultural? Or just as a multi-tool problem-solver?

You can put whatever spin you want, it's your brand. But a few of the major labels stick out to me when looking at books. Let's have a look at how not to hate falling into those buckets.

How not to hate being in the "comedy creative" box

Steve Martin famously said, "Comedy is the art of making people laugh without making them puke."[1] That one-liner is funnier than most commercials. Why? Because making people laugh is really hard, especially with a brand attached. So for anyone out there who chooses to be a "comedy creative" – good on you. It's a tough road, but a really fun one if you can pull it off. Find the agencies and brands that want it, then go make people puke.

I've worked on my share of comedy briefs, but it was always work for me. Back in the day, before I got briefed for the first time to write a round of ESPN "This is SportsCenter" (TISC) spots, I was given a DVD of every single TISC spot produced. There were over 300 of them at the time and I watched them all. This was not a hard ask. That campaign was an all-time favorite of mine, and one reason I was so excited to be at WKNY. Writing on that campaign was a dream come true. As someone for whom comedy doesn't come super naturally, I needed to get my head around the campaign format and what's been done before. You think watching 300+ spots is a lot? Consider how many scripts it took each round, and how many jokes the CDs and clients had heard throughout the years.

If you naturally excel at comedy, in advertising or otherwise, embrace it. Keep hurling your hilarious outlook on life onto your CDs and clients. The industry (and the world) is a better place when you make us laugh. And not just once a year at the Super Bowl, which has become about as funny as a

Figure 3.2 Ogilvy's hilarious "Cera-Ve" Super Bowl prank campaign. Courtesy of Alex Hold, GCD.

pharma commercial, save for Ogilvy's amazing Michael CeraVe Super Bowl spot. That was comedic genius (Figure 3.2).

If you want to be branded as a comedy creative, go forth. There will be brands to work on and agencies that need you. "I love that I get to work with hilariously angry people," Alison Gragnano (The New School, Ogilvy, Saatchi&Saatchi), ECD/Writer. Make sure everyone at the agency knows you're the funny one. When you get the right brief, go for comedy gold. Make us almost puke.

How not to hate being an "emotional" creative

All creatives are emotional. It's what makes us good at what we do. But this isn't about being emotional while creating, but creating work that evokes an emotional response. But be careful, emotion, like comedy, is very subjective and a high bar to reach.

A video I helped create while at BBDO for the final pitch presentation of the American Red Cross made everyone in the room cry, including me. And I knew what was coming! It literally still chokes me up, but that's because it was raw as all hell. One week before the final pitch, tornadoes tore through Alabama, demolishing homes like a bomb had gone off. I flew down with a barebones documentary crew from the production company "m ss ng p c s" to capture the devastation, interview survivors, and experience the Red Cross in action (Figure 3.3). It was a truly heart-wrenching experience I'll never forget. Cut to the final meeting when we played the video. Cue the waterworks.

Figure 3.3 American Red Cross winning pitch video created while at BBDO. Provided by the author.

After we won I remember thinking, "We're screwed. Now we have to make them cry every time." So let this be your warning. If you want to be the "emotional creative" get ready to find new ways to have clients cutting onions. Maybe take an acting class on learning to cry on cue? Listen to "It's Quiet Uptown" from Hamilton on repeat.

How not to hate telling people your brand is creating soulful work

Easy. Just say someone else said it. That's what I do. Fresh out of ad school, circa 2002, I was told my work had "soul" by Kevin Proudfoot, ACD/ Writer at WKNY at the time. Kevin went on to become co-ECD of WKNY alongside Todd Waterbury. He hired me about three years after we first met. So, thank you Kevin. I didn't even have to come up with my sales pitch, he did it for me. Soul isn't mutually exclusive with "emotional," but it is an indicator of some deeper insight or feeling present in the work. And that's something I don't hate to say about my own brand.

How not to hate being the cool, edgy, social-first, tech-minded creative unicorn

If someone is looking for this kind of creative, they mean someone who is into street art, or basketball, has a lot of tattoos, or knows all the latest trends. Not the ones you just pitched to your client. Those are old. They know the new, new ones. This kind of creative knows how to crack whatever we're calling the teenage audience at any given time. They are in fact unicorns because their brand has as much to do with an insight or connection to an audience, as it does with the creative output that reaches that audience.

If this is you, you probably don't hate being called this at all. Because you have something the older, more senior people at the agency don't have, and wouldn't be able to work or study hard enough to acquire. They need you for your cultural cache, your street cred, and to take all ten of your fingers on the pulse and put them on a keyboard to break the Internet. And they need you to bring all of that to a chemistry check next Tuesday. Remember to wear those cool, retro shoes you just copped.

How not to hate just being a problem-solver

The easiest way to achieve this is to specialize in being a generalist. The more helpful way is to tailor your portfolio based on the opportunity ahead. If they need a Super Bowl creative, put your biggest broadcast work first. If they need a writer for a sports brand pitch, lead with your Nike, Adidas, Under Armour or ESPN work. If they want an activation creative…you get the idea. If you don't want to get put in a box, have enough work that lives outside of it. Or just be the one thing everyone loves to have around – a business problem-solver.

Figure 3.4 Steve Conner. CEO, Fluid Content.

The first person to take a chance on me as a young, hungry junior creative in 2002, Steve Conner, now CEO of Fluid Content, has a clear perspective on this. "I don't walk in the room being a black creative, I just walk in the room being a marketing and ad guy." He punctuated the point with a story of when he was running Burrell Communications in Chicago. After a meeting with a big, blue-chip brand, during which Steve stepped way out of his lane and sold the client on an idea outside of Burrell's scope, almost certainly stepping on the toes of the brand's Agency of Record (AOR), Steve's colleague asked him, "What are you doing? We're their Black agency." To which Steve swiftly replied, "I don't know what that means. We're their agency. I'm here to solve a problem."

Sell, baby. Sell.

"I know it feels gross to promote yourself. But the market is crowded, so if you have work or you are a name people are familiar with, you're more likely to get your emails and inquiries returned." – Greg Hahn.

I wasn't sure Greg Hahn would answer "What advice do you give creatives on selling themselves?" because it's something creatives don't usually feel good talking about or admitting the importance of selling themselves. The work is always supposed to speak for itself. Like Hahn said, it felt gross. But more than that, it's because creatives could hide behind the work since so many people had to contribute to it. So if it sucks, you're not to blame. If it's great, you're part of the team (and probably taking most of the credit). But if self-promotion fails, you're all alone, and you look and feel like a fool. If it succeeds, you might feel like a cocky braggart.

Rory Hill added to the point "Certainly in the U.K. market, it's sort of sneered upon to talk about oneself." He's a Brit, and a recruiter, so he would know.

We live in a very different world today. One where self-promotion is table stakes and often, right up there with the work. Why do you think so many creatives start podcasts? It's not because they want to be Marc Maron or Conan O'Brien. It's because people remember the messenger as much as the message. Creatives today are more open to selling themselves to try and remain relevant. Unless you're pumping out a new campaign every other week, you need other ways to get your POV into the world. Whether that's via a podcast, or thought leadership, or just recalling an old production story on LinkedIn while tagging everyone in the story. It's all selling.

But don't mistake the selling for the product. In the end, something like this isn't going to be the deciding factor when hiring, according to Hill. "You don't have to start a podcast. Anything like that that's done purely to get a job nine times out of 10 is going to fail."

How not to hate selling yourself

Remember, you are not only an advertising man or woman. You are the advertisement now. Learn it. Know it. Live it. By the time this book hits your hands, that may not sound earth-shattering. It's becoming more normalized every day, so I'm guessing your reaction when reading this will hopefully be, "Duh."

Anjali Rao, CD/Writer (72andSunny, McKinney, Pereira O'Dell, FCB) agrees. "Advertising is self-promoting in a different cloak. There's (always) an Anjali wrapper I bring to the room." How you do it and live with yourself is a sliding scale. But there are some simple steps you can take that aren't all self-promotional posts on LinkedIn or Instagram.

Figure 3.5 Anjali Rao, CD, Writer.

Rework your website

Your site needs a makeover. I have never even seen it, and I know it. You're a busy creative, so you don't put that much effort into it until someone calls you about a job. Sure, you may update a new campaign here or there, but the odds are your design is stuck in the past. As you know from working in this business, the past isn't ten years ago. The past is six months ago. Or yesterday. But don't listen to me. Listen to Ferris Buehler. "Life moves pretty fast. If you don't stop and look around once in a while, you could miss it." Update your website – that's the tweet.

Get a better headshot

The cameras we have access to today are insane. You don't really need a professional headshot anymore. Just a phone, a simple backdrop, and a lighting setup. You probably know (or maybe you are) an art director with a photography hobby/problem/addiction. Use their gear, or have them take it. There's no reason to not have a good headshot. You probably also know a re-toucher from a job you just did for Huggies. Ask them to make your skin look like a baby's butt. Advertising isn't acting, but it also kind of is. You should be updating your headshot every few years. There's no reason not to.

Up your LinkedIn game

You need a LinkedIn strategy. We all do. Put a posting schedule in the calendar on your phone. Set the alert to "At time of event" and don't hit snooze. Repetition is the key to engagement. Feed the algorithm to stay in people's feeds. Again, it may sound "gross" but it works. Tag everyone involved in the post. It spreads the message far and wide. And vary up what you're posting about – new work, commentary on someone else's work, an old story that gained relevance today, an award you won, and so on. Don't be the person who only posts that you're on some jury in some awards show. No one likes that person. And don't only post when you're available for work, that doesn't work.

Be the brand, Danny

You don't need to lock yourself away in a room and come up with a whole brand campaign for yourself. You don't have to write a manifesto or a tagline. You don't have to commit anything to writing at all (except on LinkedIn). You don't have to create a mood board or a treatment. You just need to figure out your voice and your brand personality and inject it into everything you do professionally. Figure out the wrapper you put on before you enter the room. That includes your website, the work you promote, and your social posts. It's all a performance. Portfolio pieces are album releases. Your website is your Wikipedia page that you get to write. And rewrite. Figure out your brand, then be the brand.

Easy enough, right?

Note

1 "A New Comedy Scene in Aberdeen". Becca Simon. *Aberdeen Magazine*. November/December 2016.

Chapter 4

How not to hate being the adult in the room

When I was in ad school at Brainco in Minneapolis, it was 2001 and I was incredibly lucky to have the hottest agency in the world right down the street – Fallon. This was the BMW Films, Buddy Lee, Time Magazine era. No one could touch Fallon. I was also incredibly lucky that a classmate of mine named Chuck Matzer worked at Fallon at that time. He was in the studio while working on his portfolio to become an AD and we would often meet at the agency after hours to concept for the class.

What a dream it was to be in the same building as David Lubars, Greg Hahn (I didn't tell either of them I was secretly invading the office when we worked together at BBDO), and Bob Barrie. Who is Bob Barrie? That was literally the last question on the Fallon internship application. When I filled it out, I didn't have a clue. Needless to say, I didn't get the internship. But I did get the chance to peek into Bob's office and admire his stacks upon stacks of trophies. (If you're reading this Bob, don't hate Chuck).

At the time, there wasn't a more awarded creative in the world. At least, not to my knowledge. What impressed me more than his piles of hardware was how he spent 23 years at Fallon as an Art Director, not advancing to CD despite being one of the best creatives on the planet. Talk about keeping it real. He eventually found his way to the top by starting his own agency in Minneapolis and was inducted into the One Club Hall of Fame in 2024. But Bob's years at Fallon showed a real dedication to staying close to the work that's admirable.

For a similar dedication story, but different motivation, take my late father-in-law Ken Flint, a longtime JWT copywriter of the Mad Men era and beyond. He was a total hippie who saw CDs as "the man," and he never wanted to become an authority figure. That's why Ken remained a copywriter his entire career. One night after more than a few whiskeys, he told me to take a CD promotion the first chance I got. "Don't make the same mistake I made," he said. I'm pretty sure he wanted that position for me because, well, I was sharing a life with his daughter. But I also think I saw a glimmer of "what might have been" in his eye. Either way, I needed

DOI: 10.4324/9781032615707-4

convincing about as much as I needed another glass of whiskey. But thanks for the refill and revelry, Ken Flint. A true original, RIP.

Take all precautions before climbing ladder

Like I said, I didn't need the convincing. I wanted to become a CD for the same reason I think a lot of senior creatives want it, because that's just the trajectory, right? That's just what you're supposed to do. You put in your time, and then you get bumped up. Or you create a killer piece of work and get recruited to another shop. That's just what you're supposed to do, right? Well, sure. If that's your chosen path. And sometimes, even when it's not.

Julie Rutigliano (Pereira O'Dell, Fallon, McCann, JWT), ECD/Writer, remembers begging Joyce King Thomas, legendary CCO at McCann (one of the creatives behind Mastercard's "Priceless" campaign), not to make her a CD for the first time when she was at McCann in the early 2000s. "Me? Are you sure? I'm 27 years old. I'm barely an adult!" she recalls saying. "I didn't ask for it, and I got it very young. Almost to the point where it shocked me." It's shocking to me now to hear a creative admit she's not ready. That just doesn't happen anymore, in my experience. Maybe it's a generational thing? Maybe it's a Julie thing? I don't know.

Figure 4.1 Julie Rutigliano. ECD, Writer.

Ida Gronblom made a similar point and took it one step further.

> When you make that jump, you have to be so ready for it, because you don't get to do the fun stuff anymore. I've accepted that my role as a creative leader is to solve problems. It's not to be super creative.

But that transition isn't easy, and it's also not handled at the same pace as it was when she and I were coming up. "I think we're doing a lot of people an injustice right now by promoting too soon. Our generation, it happened later. For us, we were probably more ready for it."

In my experience, just about every senior creative that's ever worked for me has asked to be promoted to CD any chance they get. I remember asking one senior writer why she wanted it and she couldn't really answer. This is no knock on her – she's brilliant and grew into the role nicely – but she couldn't say why she wanted it. Why? I have a theory. It's because creatives only *think* they want to become a CD. But they don't really know what becoming one is until they get there.

So, I'm gonna tell you.

How not to hate moving from creative to creative leader

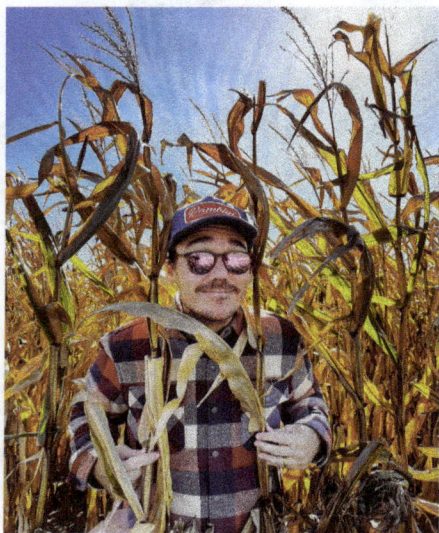

Figure 4.2 Kurt Lenard. GCD, Art Director.

What is it like to jump from being the worker to the manager? For Kurt Lenard (Digitas, BBDO, W+K), GCD/Art Director, said

it was a shock jumping into leadership because it truly doubles your work load. You have the same creative responsibilities but now you're tasked with managing up, down, personalities, egos, relationships etc. The days of being "just" a creative seem easy now.

For me, it was like becoming a parent. And a teacher, a head coach, a therapist, a doctor, a motivational speaker, a car salesman, a fireman, and MacGyver. All at the same time. While getting dressed, in public. Oh, I almost forgot, it's also about being a great judge of creative. Can't forget the creative part! But don't for a second think that's the main part. In my experience, that's the first misconception rising CDs make. They think they're just going to just sit on a throne and judge work all day. So when they realize it's so much more, that's where some hate might creep in.

The second? They think they're being handed the keys to the castle. Sometimes that's true, sometimes not. The reality is the CD role varies depending on the agency. My first CD job at BBDO was little more than a title. I was given no business to run or team to lead. I was basically a

Figure 4.3 "Disappearing Agents" spot from Translation. Directed by Roman Coppola. Courtesy of the author.

well-paid Senior Creative. Not a bad thing if that's what you want, but not great if you want to play more of a leadership role.

My first real chance at leading a big client came as CD of State Farm at Translation (Figure 4.1). It was a huge piece of business with almost the entire creative department reporting to me at any given time, and tons of client face time. CD level = unlocked.

And I'll never forget what my CCO at Translation John Norman told me about leading creatives. He said it's like teaching them to read the book "See Spot Run." I didn't completely understand what he meant at the time, but I do now. It means creatives are children. Kidding! Kind of. It means… Be direct. Be clear. Keep it simple. Assume they know nothing.

So that's it? Chapter over? Not a chance. Here's a beginner's guide to becoming a creative leader. Notice I didn't say "Director." That's just the title. Leader is the job.

Step #1: Get over yourself

This isn't about you anymore. I know, I know. You just got this big new promotion or position based on your ideas and talent and all that. Plus, everyone's looking at you and you're holding the keys to the castle, so it has to kind of be about you, right? Nope. Sorry. No matter how much you want this to be. It's not. Get over yourself. You've made your point. You got the title. You got the account. Now it's your job to make sure the creatives (and agency and clients) get the best possible work made. Your name is going on the work anyway.

Tell me if you've heard a creative say this, or said it yourself: *Is this the kind of idea that (Insert CD/ECD/CCO name here) will like?* Ack! This has to stop. And as a creative leader, you can stop it. You're not there to be catered to. You're there to help, lead, and inspire. The brief wasn't written to please you. It was written to solve a business problem. The creatives coming up with the ideas should first be trying to please themselves and then get YOU on board with why it's great – in service of that business problem.

Figure 4.4 RicardoViramontes. CCO/Art Director.

Legendary music and cultural guru Rick Rubin made a similar point in his book *The Creative Act: A Way of Being*, when he said, "In terms of priority, inspiration comes first. You come next. The audience comes last."

As the CD, you are the first "audience" of the work. But don't make it about pleasing you. This is probably one of the single most difficult parts of making the transition to upper management. But you can do it.

Ricardo Viramontes (AirBnB, Spring Hill, Apple, Lyft, CAA, W+K), a CCO whose career has taken him to some of the most creative companies in the world described it like this. "You've been an individual contributor up to this point. Now it's not about you. It's about them. Create an environment for people to feel safe to wield their power."

How not to hate it being about someone else for a change

1 Ask your creatives what they need help with, then help them. Simple as that.
2 Send your creatives to a meeting, or a presentation, or a shoot, instead of you.
3 Go teach a class. You'll learn more from your students than they'll learn from you.
4 Take improv. You'll be reminded about the sum of the parts.
5 Have kids. You'll instantly realize where you stand in the world.

Step #2: Watch what you say

In advertising, words matter. Imagine if W+K pitched "Let's do it" instead of "Just do it" or Goodby and Silverstein presented "Get some milk" instead of "Got milk?" Again, words matter. And when you rise to management, they matter more than ever before. So choose your words very carefully. Yes, yes, of course, everything you've ever said was always completely profound and meaningful (just ask your mom!). But now, your words make big things happen. Like, deciding what work goes to the client and what gets held back. Who does or doesn't get a bonus? Whether someone has to work the weekend, or not.

But first, let's clear something up quick...

This section is not talking about watching what you say in a DE&I or HR context, yet both of those should absolutely be of concern. And if you need this book to spell out why, then I'm afraid you may not be ready for leadership. You can keep reading, but you know, for future reference. For the rest of you...

This section is about the weight your words carry in leadership with creatives, internal teams, people above you, with clients, across the industry, and thanks to the internet, in perpetuity. So if you're more of a "ready, shoot, aim" type of leader, this might be a tough pill to swallow. It's not meant to scare you from speaking your mind, just to be that little voice on your shoulder who also wears cool sneakers and maybe a trucker hat, reminding you to be mindful of what dribbles out of your mouth hole.

If you're a reasonably well-adjusted person (in advertising?), measure twice, cut once type, who has now been entrusted by an agency to lead business and mentor creatives, this will come with a certain degree of latitude, particularly if you're new to it. Also, since you're a creative. So you can, and should, say dumb stuff. I say dumb stuff all the time. But it's usually about the work. Like, when I wonder if we can get Steven Spielberg to direct a TikTok campaign. Or if the White House is a viable production location. That's the good dumb stuff. Do more of that. Do less of the dumb stuff that makes you actually appear stupid. Nobody actually wants a stupid CD, even if the mannequin that greets you at W+K London reception says, *Walk in stupid every day.*

So how can you not hate saying the wrong thing?

1 Take passive language out of your vocabulary. Instead of "I think maybe we don't need a TV spot" say "We don't need a TV spot."
2 Never make a promise you can't keep. For example, don't say to a Senior Copywriter asking to be promoted to ACD, "I'm definitely planning to

promote you. I just need time." Unless you already put in that request and are literally waiting for finance to approve it.

3 Get used to saying no. It's a lot easier to change a "no" to a "yes" than vice versa.
4 Be intentional. "I don't hate it" is not the same as "I love it."
5 Stop saying "That's what I would do." It's just a passive-aggressive way of saying "Do it my way."
6 Say "What do you think?" before saying "Here's what I think."

Step #3: Be decisive

Did Coach Shooter Flatch in the movie *Hoosiers* know the picket fence was going to work in dying seconds? In the movie *A Few Good Men*, did Lt. Daniel Kaffee know Col. Jessup would admit to ordering the code red when he said he wanted the truth? Am I going to use any other examples that aren't from 1980s or 1990s movies? No. No. And probably not. The thing is, sometimes you just have to run a ridiculous play or accuse a four-star general of a crime, even if it's not the safe or best choice. Make the bold choice, and then own it.

You won't make the right decision every time. You're going to make some bad choices. Not wrong choices, but bad ones. You are also going to make some brilliant choices. Hopefully more so than the bad ones. The most important thing is that you *make* a decision, early, and believe in it. Nobody likes a waffler, especially in leadership.

The decision could be only going to a pitch with one idea instead of three. It could mean pushing for a sizzle in the eleventh hour instead of reading a manifesto. It could be not showing the safe idea at all. Better to be decisive and wrong than indecisive and lost.

Make a call. Be firm. And run with it. Just don't be a jerk or inflexible about it, and you'll see. People will run with you. Behind you. Next to you. And eventually past you, on the way to the finish line.

It might be hard. Many creatives aim to please and they want people to like them and their ideas. But great creative leaders are a little more of the *The Art of Not Giving a F****** type than the *How to win friends and influence people* type.

How not to hate owning your decisions

1 Stick to your guns. You might be wrong, but you won't seem unsure.
2 If you are wrong, admit it. You'll get a lot of respect for owning up to it.
3 Call the client. Take the blame. They'll trust you next time.
4 The more conviction you show, the less explanation is required.
5 Have a reco when the client asks. Don't waffle if they don't agree.

Step #4: Protect the work

This might be the hardest part of the job and an easy one to hate. You thought recognizing the idea, then blowing the idea out, then crafting the hell out of the idea was hard. Then you realize yet another part of your new job description – protecting the work. That means protecting it internally before it goes to clients, then from clients once they like the idea. Because once they like it – watch out – changes are coming.

It means protecting it from partner agencies trying to change it, with the Media company trying to retrofit it to their plan. It means protecting the work after the budget gets cut and after research comes back. For months and months.

Take it from a hockey goalie. Or a soccer goalie. Or someone on the firing line. It's a lot easier to be the one doing the shooting than it is getting shot at. But you need to take the bullets and keep the idea moving.

How not to hate protecting the work

1 A mediocre idea will take as much time as a great idea.
2 Continually remind everyone why they loved the idea in the first place.
3 Get used to saying, "trust me" if they need someone to blame. Or "blame me" if they still don't want to trust you.
4 Decide which details can be changed without losing the idea.
5 Come up with another idea to prove why this idea is the right one.
6 Don't say "we'll try it" unless you genuinely think it can work. Because if you try it, they'll want it.
7 Be ready to walk away from the idea. Protecting an idea can also mean not letting the wrong people ruin it.

HATERADE
GET IT OUT OF YOU

Designer: Bryan Haker

Step #5: Care about the people as much as you care about the work

Clients come and go. Pitches are won and lost. CMOs leave. Your favorite client could get fired while you're on an airplane on the way to present to him. Then that same client could be your colleague a month later when the agency hires him. (This happened) The point is – we work in a finicky business that doesn't care how you think you're being treated. But you know who does care about how they're treated? The people in the fight with you are getting pummeled like drum heads in the movie *Whiplash*. Big fancy awards may get you your next job. But caring about people will get them to follow you there. And anywhere else you end up.

"I find it very hard to make great creative work if you don't care about the people making it. I know that sounds corny and I hate myself for saying it. But it's true," said Julie Rutigliano.

How not to hate taking care of your people

1 Treat them like people, not just idea machines. Does this really have to be said? Sadly, yes.
2 Pay for dinner. Even if you can't expense it. You were hungry once, too.
3 Check-in with them before they come to you.
4 Go to the internal and let the creatives do the talking. Your silence will show confidence in them and conviction in the work.
5 Insist your creatives are in the client presentation. It's their work. They should share it.
6 Leave them alone at night and on the weekends. Unless clear expectations have been set for late night or weekend work, it can wait.

Again, Ricardo Viramontes said it best.

You have to really, really care. You're now responsible for somebody's livelihood. Everyone has a parent, or a partner, or a mortgage. Your brain switches to the responsibility for those people. When they go home what are they saying about you?

Heavy stuff. But I never said it would be easy.

Step #6: You're a leader, so lead

Creative leaders need to lead the entire creative process. Not just on the work, but who works on the work. Who's right for the brief and who isn't? To know and make those decisions, quickly. If you don't have the right resources for the project, ask for freelance. You'll be the one making the case to the CFO, so make it good. It's their job to make the agency money, not give it to you. And you thought you'd only be using the power of persuasion with clients? Ha.

When it's time to hire, you'll lead that process, too. You'll have recruiters and others helping, but ultimately the decision should be yours. Ask around. Look back through emails from creatives or friend recommendations.

Research work you admire and go after those creatives. Hiring is one of the most important things you'll do as a creative leader. Half of leading is what you do when everyone else is working.

Get used to saying things like... *Let me share you on a deck I started to show you what I mean.*

Leading can also mean getting your hands dirty and writing or rewriting the deck yourself. Give it a narrative, not just creative ideas. A narrative is a story and you are a storyteller. Then, get in a room with strategy and beat up the narrative until it's rock solid. Writing the deck will help you determine what work to take to the client. While creatives are writing up their ideas, creative leaders are writing a narrative to sell those ideas.

And... *We just finished the presentation. The work presented really well. Thanks for making me and the whole team look so smart.*

Leading is sending the email to the whole team after a big presentation to say thank you to everyone who killed themselves on it. This must come the same day. It doesn't matter if you're running to make the last train back from Philly to NYC and just want to collapse in your seat, or huddle with Account and Strat in the bar car – send the email. It can be three sentences (see above). If you couldn't get your creatives to the presentation, they at least need an e-pat on the back.

How not to hate taking the lead

1 Get a career coach. Everyone can use more advice and practice.
2 Go shopping. If you look like a leader, you'll feel like one.
3 Set up regular check-ins with creatives and CDs. And don't cancel them.
4 If it's your meeting, you start it. If it isn't, don't.
5 Skip some meetings all together. Leadership can also mean letting others lead.

Step #7: Buy a scarf

Kidding, not kidding. Not the kind of scarf you wear because it's 10° out. The kind you wear indoors, in the summer, to look, you know, creative. Like a big-time CD. Not into scarves? Fine, get a hat. A trucker hat. A bowler. A fedora. A stocking cap that's too big so you let it hang off the back of your head. A cycling cap with Rapha imprinted on the flipped up brim. Don't like hats? Ok, then get some tattoos. Or piercings. Or grow a beard. Or better yet, a mustache! Or a black turtleneck. Or oversized, blue tortoise shell-rimmed glasses. Or load up on ironic 80s rock t-shirts. Or dye your hair purple. Got the look for you? Great. You did it. You reached the Google images results of "creative leader" status.

But seriously, I am not an indoor scarf person. I'm not even much of an outdoor scarf person. Nothing against anyone who likes, owns, or wears any of the above. Just be you. You're in the spotlight now. People want a creative leader who is confident in their style and aware of their image. That image could include a jumpsuit. Or bib overalls. Or Paris St. Germain Jordan 5s. Or, say you really like Prince t-shirts. Then, good for you. Go crazy! But remember this: none of this is going to make you more creative. But plenty of things can make you feel and appear more confident. Whatever your thing is, own it.

My wife often says, you can never overdress and she's mostly right. Although, "dressing up" means something much different in advertising. But what she means is people will notice if you're too dressed down more than too dressed up. I wore a full suit to the holiday party one year when it wasn't required. And you know what? I was the only one who did, but damn I looked good. And shouldn't a leader wear a suit once in a while, if for no other reason than to keep the Mad Men dream alive? Ken Flint would say so.

Speaking of Mad Men, what about the Don Drapers of the world

Ok, so far this has all been about becoming a CD. But what about leveling up to, say GCD? Or ECD? Or Global ECD? Or the top of the top, CCO? You've learned to manage teams, lead accounts, probably even a creative department, and worked across all other departments. How different could the next level be? Is it still not about you? Yes. It's still not about you (get over it). But everyone will want a piece of you, so it can be challenging to retain a sense of self. As they say, it's lonely at the top.

When you rise to the highest level of creative leadership in your agency, you are not just a senior creative leader. You're much more than a creative. You will wear more hats than you have hooks to hang them.

Before Sean Bryan (McCann, DDB, JWT) became a CCO, he thought the job would be what it looked like as a creative. "I would go into the CCO's office and show them stuff and they would pick stuff, like, ideas one, three and seven." So he thought it was a "pick your favorite stuff job." But, "that's the tail, not the dog. You need to understand all the businesses and relationships you're now in charge of, how to build a culture, maintain morale, fend off CFOs...*then* pick the good stuff." Basically, "it's a totally different job."

How not to hate your "totally different job"? Compare it to other totally different jobs! Being a CCO or ECD is kinda like being a...

Firefighter

Your job is to put out fires. Big, eleventh hour about to lose a client fires. Smaller, creatives missed an internal deadline again fires. And medium-sized, a CD pissed off an account person type fires. Sometimes, this is all you do all day. And like real fires, you can't control when they happen. You need to be ready to toss on your helmet, grab a hose, and put out the flames.

Game show host

You and Pat Sajak are basically the same now (just maybe less Botox?). You too are performing day in and day out before a live audience. You need to be camera-ready. You're supposed to know all the answers. You are full of witty things to say. You hand out large sums of money to people. You always have Vanna White at your side…ok, maybe not that one.

Career coach

Wait, didn't we just say you needed a career coach? Surprise! You are also going to be one, you'll be guiding people's careers as much as their creative work.

Professional sports coach

You will be surrounded by some of the best talent in the world, at the top of their game. While they are training and honing their skills, you will be orchestrating and creating a game plan for their success.

Behavioral therapist

Creatives don't know how to get all of their assignments done and also go pee. It's amazing how much this will come up. It's your job to give them the tools to get through these obstacles. Even if that literally means telling them to put a block on their calendar to take a whiz. Or stalling a meeting for five minutes until they're back.

President of the United States (of advertising)

Your schedule will be triple booked. You'll be briefed on everything. And everything will be hugely important. Your iPhone will become a Cold War Red Phone. You'll have to win hearts and minds. And hopefully, if you give a rousing presentation in a packed conference room, you'll get a standing ovation.

Still want to become a creative leader? Even if you kind of hate how vastly different it will be than you imagined? Sure, you do. Don't hate the position. Hate the game. Actually, don't hate that either. That's the whole point of this book…

Growing up pains

"If you look around the table and can't tell who the sucker is, it's you." This is a famous saying in poker. Who actually coined it is debatable, but this isn't a poker book. The same point could be made about the "responsible adult" in advertising. One day you look around and realize, *Oh man, that's me.* It doesn't make you a sucker. But it is a sobering moment. Don't freak out. This was inevitable. In fact, you want it to happen. It means you're still in the business and successful. And now, you have some actual power and say-so.

Ok, so you're no longer the cool, young, recklessly creative wild child anymore. But you don't suddenly forget how to write a great headline or knock out an amazing comp. You'll just use those muscles a little less, but not entirely depending on the structure of where you work. That's the growing pains part. Instead of getting briefed and then left alone for half a day, you'll now be in a bunch of meetings. You may no longer be the beacon of what's cool in the world, but people will now wait for you to start a meeting. Which isn't a terrible place to be.

You'll have a lot of feelings about this change at first. When you realize no one's looking to you for the deets on the latest PALACE collab or KITH drop. Or whether people are even saying "deets" anymore (They are not). But this is what you always wanted, right? To get a seat at the table and be taken seriously not just as a creative, but as a professional problem solver, leader, and mentor? Assuming this is the case, and you're not in the wrong meeting, let's talk about what this step means.

Fine, so you're now the adult in the room. The responsible one. The wise one. The one they come to for all the answers to all of their questions. Like vacation requests (*He wants to go to New Zealand for how long?*) and salary raise requests (*Didn't we just give this person a raise like 4 months ago?*) and more requests for more responsibility (*But they can't even handle their current projects, how can they take on more?*). And so many, many more.

Well done, pal. CUT TO: a pat on the back. People now trust you enough to put you in this position. And you get to make a bunch of new decisions. Fun decisions, like what furniture you should order for the new office space (*I like the bean bags more than the noodle chairs.*). Small decisions, like who gets briefed on the DCO banners. (*Give it to the new guy.*) Decisions you never wanted to make (*We have to lose one FTE, who is it?*). And huge decisions you can't believe they're letting you make (*Who should we hire as the new Managing Director?*)

You might feel weird about it at first, but you won't hate it. It's what you've been working toward. Also, because you literally won't have time to hate it.

More things than you'll have time to hate

Remember when you got a driver's license and your parents handed you the keys and said, "Remember, it's not a toy. It's a big responsibility" and you said, "Ok" but actually thought "Let's go do brake stands! And tee-pee people! And blast music! And go through the Taco Bell drive thru!" This is less like that scenario, and more like when you first went to college and realized, "Shit, I have to sign for these classes myself? And no one's gonna wake me up and make me go to them? And if I don't, I'll fail?"

It's on you now. All of it. But it came along with a big promotion into management at your current agency, or at a new agency or to run a big brand or a few brands, or maybe even the whole creative department. Amazing! Congrats! Your career choices have been validated! Your hard work was worth it! Being an adult has paid off! Literally! Look at all those extra zeroes! But pretty much right away, you'll forget about those zeroes. Because you now have more to your job than ever before.

Talk to finance. Like a boss. Approve vacation days. Like a boss. Give feedback. Like a boss

Get ready to have not just more say-so in the work, but more sway with clients. More pushback power. More new biz chemistry checks. More meetings where you give people bonuses. More meetings with HR that have nothing to do with bad behavior. More meetings, period. Plus, more insight into the business itself. How it works. When it doesn't. What EBITDA means (Earnings Before Interest, Taxes, Depreciation, and Amortization). How scopes work. Who is covered on what account and who isn't covered at all. How much the agency spent on freelancers last year, which accounts are sucking up most of the creative department's time, while producing the least amount of profit. Really sexy stuff. Grown-up stuff. Stuff you never thought you'd care about when you were concepting the next Snickers Super Bowl campaign in a stinky room somewhere on Sixth Avenue.

And that's ok because this often happens around the time of the birth of an actual kid, too (or twins, in my case). You get hit with a lot more than you bargained for and there's no time for adjustment. You just gotta figure it out as you go. Once you've been through that, it actually makes juggling the extra workload somewhat easier, believe it or not. One, because kids have a way of forcing everyone to get organized. Even creatives. And two, because managing is a lot like parenting. That's not meant to be patronizing. It's just the truth.

Behold (clears throat) the responsible adult creative professional!

Let's take a closer look at this increasingly rare creature.

- Probably wakes up by 7 am, likely without an alarm
- Picks up phone from nightstand to check email, before stepping out of bed
- Eats (a sensible?) breakfast, knowing other meals are not guaranteed
- Puts on smartwatch, not to look cool. But for the alerts and constant communication (and maybe the ECG monitor?)
- Can handle more than five projects at a time, but often juggling double that
- Is aware of the status of every project within their purview
- Knows exactly how long it takes to write a manifesto, or concept a TVC, or whip up a new business deck
- Just whipped up a deck narrative while you were reading this
- Just hired someone
- Just fired someone
- Is waiting on approval to promote someone
- By 12 pm on any given weekday, this creature has already judged an awards show, went to a chem-check, presented a new brand platform, and texted a client to pre-sell their favorite idea in a deck that's about to be presented
- At 12:35, they congratulated the team for selling that idea

But it's not all approvals and happy hours. There's one last topic we have to cover when it comes to moving on up, and you won't like it. Because you know it's coming for you, one day.

How not to hate ageism in advertising

James Murphy of LCD Soundsystem wrote an entire song on this topic titled, "Losing my edge" that could just as well be about aging in advertising. If you know, you know. If you don't, pull it up on Spotify or Google the lyrics. If you don't yet relate to them, congrats! You're still the one with an edge. For those who find that song painfully relatable, you're not alone, and you're not imagining it. Ageism is a real problem in advertising that's just sitting there at a slow boil on the back burner, ready to be served to anyone who hits the magical age of (don't say it!) 50 years old. (don't say it again!) That's right, 50 years old.

Finally, a topic that's okay to hate in this book! Right? Well, yes and no. Because yes, it's a prevalent issue that doesn't appear to be going away. But also no, because getting older isn't something you can control. No matter how many Dove beauty products you buy or Peloton classes you join.

Age 50 is the proverbial albatross hanging over every creative's neck from the moment they get their first job, whether they want to admit it or not. Most of those I speak to do in fact admit it, but then also admit that they don't know what to do about it.

In advertising, we're constantly being asked to sell to an audience that will never grow older, because there will always be another generation (Millennials, Gen Z, Gen Alpha...). While those of us doing the selling are slowly marching ourselves toward irrelevance with every year of experience. It can start to feel like the more you become an expert, the less valuable you become. Experience today seems to be seen more as an expensive hindrance, than an invaluable asset. Why pay a senior expert when a junior, or even AI, can do it cheaper and faster?

I don't write this to bum anyone out, or to be self-serving as someone just shy of that dreaded advertising age of death. I bring it up because it's something I've known to be true since taking my first job at MTV, a place that always makes you feel your age. I also don't pretend to have all the answers, but do think there are ways to turn a blind eye to the hate, or at least laugh in its face.

The following ideas won't fix the system, but may help you navigate through it

1 Remember that your ideas are what keeps you relevant, not your age. If you're holding a black pencil or a titanium lion, no one cares that you're not on the 30 under 30 list.
2 Hire experienced creatives if you're in a position to do so. Be the solution, not the problem.
3 Send agency-wide emails about relevant trends and topics. Remind the youth that you got your finger on the pulse.
4 Judge awards shows and speak on industry panels. Put your years of experience to good use.
5 Start your own agency. No one can age you out of your own place. And if they do, at least you'll be laughing your way to the bank.
6 Stay connected to culture. Don't be the one saying "Is that a font?" when someone brings up Ariana Grande.

Don't become the leader you hated

Being a great creative doesn't automatically translate to being a great CD. "He or she is a great creative, but a terrible manager." I would hear this from creatives at a bunch of different agencies, and it was something I never wanted to be said about me. It seemed like such an easy trap to fall into. Can write, can't teach. Can create, can't coach. Only focusing on the creative, not the leadership part. Becoming the adult in the room is great, but it isn't for everyone. We wouldn't have Jackass the Movie if every crazy kid grew up to become a well-adjusted adult. This chapter can't save you from becoming your parents. But it can save you from becoming that CD you hated and never wanted to be.

Chapter 5

How not to hate your current job

Jobs are hard, to land and to stay interested in. Just look at LinkedIn. Actually, don't. It's not a healthy way to spend your time. When you work in an industry where being at the same job for, say, four years is considered "a long time" you need to be okay with change. Contrast that with my parents' generation (Boomers), a time when most people had the same job for 30+ years. Whether they hated it or not wasn't the point. They had secure employment, backed by unions with good pensions and seniority. When I got laid off, I think my mom took it harder than I did.

I'll never forget when I got a call from a recruiter only two months into my new job at a Translation. She wanted to see if I was surviving and to run a new opportunity past me. "Too soon," I said. I don't think I'd even had filled out my 401k form yet. I hadn't even had the chance to hate my job yet. In the end, I only stayed 18 months. Some people last three months there, so I felt like a lifer. This wasn't unique to that agency. Since then, I've worked at four other agencies in ten years. That's just how the industry works. In some rare cases, people stick around at an agency for the long haul, moving up through management and making a lifelong career. But most creatives jump around, looking for new opportunities and experiences. That's part of the fun of our business.

Easy come, easy go somewhere else

The teachers at my portfolio school would constantly tell students to "follow the work." Great advice indeed. For me, I always followed my impulse to do something I hadn't done yet. Starting off at MTV, I mainly worked on print. So I went to W+K and worked primarily on TV. After that, I felt an urge to work at a huge agency to work on huge brands, so I went to BBDO. After a few years, I felt the need to get scrappy again and went to Translation. And so on, and so on.

DOI: 10.4324/9781032615707-5

For me, jumping around wasn't out of dissatisfaction, but out of curiosity. I think some people are looking to find a permanent home. But I've been more interested in fulfilling some kind of need within myself more than anything. I have friends at W+K who were there when I got hired and are still there. Same for MTV. And those jobs were decades ago. So it is possible to find "the one" and settle down. But a lot of us in the business are jumpers and that's okay. How you get from point **A**rts & Letters to point **B**SSP to point **C**rispin is up to you. When you go (or don't) is what we're here to talk about.

Should you stay or should you go now?

If you don't love this business and don't get a buzz from it, you won't last. It's not a clock-in-and-out kind of job. It's all-consuming. So you better love it and find joy in the chaos, otherwise, this industry is not for you.

Figure 5.1 Samira Ansari. Chief Creative Officer, Art Director.

Wise advice from Samira Ansari (Ogilvy, Deutsch, FCB), CCO. Let's take it a step further.

An early mentor of mine dropped two bits of knowledge that have stuck with me. The first one was, *If you're not learning from your CD, you don't belong there.* The second one was, *If your boss can't write a better ad than you, it's time to go.* Both are true, but not the only rubric to make your decision.

How did I know it was time to go whenever I made my different jumps? Specific details won't do the rest of my career any favors, but this list might help *you* figure it out.

1 You tell yourself you hate your job. (Welp, that was easy).
2 You tell other people you hate your job.
3 You're scrolling through LinkedIn.
4 You're scrolling through LinkedIn. A lot.
5 You're emailing recruiters.
6 You're spending more time on your portfolio than your assignments.
7 You booked a vacation without asking your boss.
8 You begin to skip creative department meetings.

9   You're off-camera a lot.
10 You hit the snooze button more often.
11 You leave the agency party early.
12 You don't go to the agency party at all.
13 You sent your boss's phone call to voicemail.
14 You go out for drinks/coffee to rant about work a few times a week.

That is not an exhaustive list. But if you've been in this situation, it can be an exhausting existence. Can your situation be saved? That depends on how many you tick off the list and whether you care to eliminate any others. Still undecided? Ask yourself, if you care enough to stay.

1   Do you want to go to the office (without a mandate)?
2   Do you get excited about briefings?
3   Do you care if your work is shared at all-agency meetings?
4   Are you asking for more responsibility? Or a promotion?
5   Do you tell your spouse/partner/mom/friends what you're working on?
6   Can you see yourself in upper management there?
7   Are you proud to tell friends where you work?

There's no scoresheet for the answers. Just asking and answering them is enough to know. If the answers aren't conclusive, or you don't like the answer, it's not too late. You can still decide not to hate your current job. We'll get to that.

But first, let's talk about money

On the topic of money, my same ad school teachers were united in their advice. They would say if you follow the work, the money will come. But if you follow the money, the work may not. They said it all the time. I got tired of hearing it. It's still great advice to this day. But let's face it, we aren't fine artists. Not everyone can follow every creative whim. We can't all get hired at (insert hottest current agency name).

If I had to guess, I'd say most of you didn't get into the business just for the money. But it's a great nice-to-have, isn't it? Anyone who pretends not to care about cashing those inflated checks every other week isn't being honest. Or hasn't been without it long enough to remember what that's like? We all start as broke creatives living off the $20 after hours dinner stipend. Maybe you still are. We go through that period for the promise that the money will come eventually. And once it does, it feels damn good. Don't forget that feeling. Even when it just becomes your normal way of living. You are very fortunate to make really good money coming up with ideas.

Making good money is exciting, and once it happened to me, I was thrilled. But honestly, I didn't even know the salary until I was already really excited about the opportunity. Then I saw the money and was like…whoa. Seeing it spelled out in black and white in an offer letter was staggering. I tried to always remember what that felt like when things get tough. Because no matter how hard we think advertising is, we get a lot of money to do a lot of different things, most of which are not that bad, like…

- Wear black t-shirts to work
- Write commercials that make people laugh
- Eat fast food, while solving problems about fast food
- Write boring things
- Write exciting things
- Write 100 headlines about motorcycle insurance
- Design a logo for a marijuana company
- Write social copy that gets ignored
- Make small talk with clients over omakase
- Present big ideas to CMOs who buy big ideas
- And yes, sometimes be asked to skip a vacation for a client presentation

When you think about the money, these things become easier. But you won't think about the money if you're a creative. You're thinking about ideas because that's what you get paid to do. That doesn't mean you can't hate your current job, even if they pay you good money. If you do, odds are it's for one of the following reasons.

How not to hate your current job if…the agency doesn't match your ambition

This may be too tough to overcome, but let's try. Can you use the job for something other than creative output? For example, getting promoted. If you set your site on getting into a more senior leadership position, that shift can help you reimagine your goals at the place. Of course, you still want to strive for creative greatness, who doesn't? But what else can you get there besides great creative?

Let's say you are an ACD and want to become a CD. What if you redirected your energy toward proving to the agency that you should be given more responsibility? Make it clear to your boss. Ask to lead more projects. Get in front of clients more often and make an impression. Organize a cultural event at the agency. Start acting like a leader and they will start seeing you as one.

Now, instead of being angry about the agency not believing in an idea you thought was brilliant, your focus is getting the agency to start believing you are brilliant. Once you are promoted, you'll be able to advocate for the work you want to make. Or you can go get another job with the experience you just gained.

How not to hate your current job if...you have a difficult client

What if the problem isn't the agency but the clients? Maybe they're difficult. Or idiots. Or complete jerks. Maybe they don't know how to say yes to a good idea, no matter how hard you try. Maybe they wouldn't know a good idea if it was staring them in the face. Maybe they always pick the safest work. The solution for that might be easier said than done, depending on where you work, but it is...DON'T BRING CLIENTS SAFE WORK. Let's assume you've fought that battle and are stuck in a tough spot, with a tough client. They don't know what they want. First, I'm sorry. This is the worst position to be in. But it's not a lost cause.

Alison Gragnano (The New School, Ogilvy, Saatchi&Saatchi, Margeotes Fertitta & Partners), ECD/Writer, has some sage advice.

> Realize clients are really scared a lot of the time and if there's a way to make the idea and the risk that they're taking less scary for them that, that's one approach. When they come into a creative presentation, they are scared shitless. A client even told me that once, it was like, 'What the hell are they gonna try to sell me today?'

So don't think of it as selling them something they don't want, but rather, making something that's good for them. Change your mindset a little bit.

Remember this: Unless your clients fell backward into their position, or are nihilistic curmudgeons who hate everything, I'd be willing to bet they went into marketing for the same reasons you did – to make amazing stuff. To put new ideas out into the world that make their friends laugh or cry. Ideas that move culture and make a huge splash. Your clients, no matter how difficult, want what you want – to make a difference. Now, their difference may not match yours. They may want to climb the ladder at their company, or earn their bonus, or please thousands of stakeholders who they need to convince that the idea you're going to make together is going to be amazing. Or they may just want to impress their spouse. Whatever their reason, also remember this: they can't do any of that without you. As the creative, you have something they need...

A great idea.

But before they can buy your great idea, you need to do the hard work of getting them used to saying yes. If you've already gone round and round, just stop. You're giving away great ideas for a frustrated client to kill. Stop the merry-go-round before you lose your lunch.

Take control

Ricardo Viramontes (AirBnB, SpringHill, Apple, Lyft, CAA, W+K), Chief Creative Officer/Art Director, had an interesting perspective on control when he said that creatives in this scenario need to ask themselves, "What can you do that's within your control? How can you make the client a hero? Have you done all the soft power things that have nothing to do with the work?" He continued, "If you're feeling like, 'Maybe I could've traveled a little more to meet them or invited them to dinner.' I wouldn't wait. It's not just the account person's responsibility." Great point. Do whatever you can to make the relationship as strong as possible.

Make the call

Call your client. Either directly, or with the account lead. Connect on a personal level. This isn't a meeting. It's a chat. They'll know you care about them succeed, not just your idea. Stop presenting and start partnering. Bring them into the process. You'll find it's a lot easier to get a bunch of little yeses along the way than waiting for a big fat NO at the end.

Whenever he finds a creative idea isn't getting through, Gary Van Dzura (BBH, W+K, R/GA) a 20+ year ECD/Art Director, advances the work by using the old school tactic of...wait for it...picking up the phone!

> I would just call (my client) one-on-one and go, 'Dude, what do you want to do?' I would do that on Fox Sports and on Jordan (brand). When you have a good relationship with the client, you can just say, 'Do we want to do this?'

Kick around ideas

If they don't have the time, then go to their team. Get them on your side. Bring them into the process. Don't take the brief and disappear for two weeks. Take the brief and call them two days later. Ask if they want to kick around some thoughts. As a creative, this can be a hard concept to wrap your head around. Your ideas and your process are your lifeblood. Your brain may not compute. *So I'm just going to concept with the client?* No. You're going to plant the seeds of the idea you want them to buy and make them think it was their idea. Its Jedi mind tricks meet Inception, and it works.

Solve it like a brief

I asked Steve Conner, CEO/Founder of Fluid Content, how he gets a difficult client on his side.

It's always the same trick. They become just another campaign that you're running, so you use the same techniques. Who are you? What do you believe? What do your friends think about you? You gotta get deep to understand who they (the client) are as an archetypal character. You got to understand what their drama is and what their goal is. What you're doing is you're selling them on what they believe to get to what it is that you know about this audience and what they believe.

But what if you have the kind of client who enjoys torturing their agency, yelling at their team, and demanding new creatives on the business every other day? These types of mercurial clients are hopefully becoming a thing of the past. But if you find yourself working for one, and your agency won't stand up for you or your team...then I think you know what to do.

How not to hate your current job if...there's no room for growth

Only you know where you want your career to go. If you find you're at an agency where there's no growth in your position, it's time to ask yourself some hard questions, like...

Would they create a new position for you?

If you're a GCD and there's already an ECD, could you be happy heading up a new department? Say, social? Or trends? Or social trends? Or maybe you want to head up a special swat team that only takes on timely projects? Or could you take on a Creative Excellence role? What about creating an entertainment division? If you can't grow up, think about growing sideways.

Can you stick it out and add to your portfolio?

Are you doing great work or winning a bunch of awards? Can you keep doing that until the right opportunity either (a) comes up at your current job, or (b) a recruiter drops an amazing opportunity in front of you? If so, just keep grinding. Stay busy. Pad your book. That is, unless you're not adding to your portfolio, well...I think you know what to do.

Can you ask what it would take to be considered in the most senior position?

It doesn't hurt to ask. In fact, it will make quitting easier if/when you do leave. There will be no question about why you're not getting what you want. If they don't ever see you in senior leadership, you need to know that. And you need to know why so you can work on that for the next position.

Can you make it until you get your bonus?

This is obviously time-sensitive, as many companies give out bonuses in Q1. But if you can wait. Great. If not, then make your peace with losing out on the loot.

Can you wait at least until the beginning of next month?

Don't quit on say, July 29th or November 30th. When you do that, you screw yourself out of a month of healthcare. Quit in the first couple of days of the month. It gives you time to find another job, or line up freelance, before your health insurance expires. Learn from my mistakes.

Can you get yourself laid off so you can collect severance?

Now, we're admittedly entering George Constanza territory here, but if you can manage to figure this one out, you are a genius. If you already want to quit and can be made redundant instead, you just won the "I hate my current job" lottery. The genius store called. They're running out of you.

How not to hate your current job if...you think the agency doesn't believe in doing big, breakthrough work

Leave, probably. Any other questions? Because I have a few, and they may help you settle this thing once and for all.

Have you asked to be part of the new business team, so you can bring in a new client that can push the client to bigger things?

If people at the agency are stopping big work from getting to the client, have you considered going directly to the client on the side?

Would that anger too many people? Is the risk worth it if it works? If not, could you steal the client and start your own shop?

Not an entrepreneur? Ok, well, is there another role you'd like at the agency?

Or do they have another office? Could you ask to be transferred?

Is the answer no to any or all of these? Well, then is your portfolio updated?

If this is you, then yes, you probably hate your current job.

How not to hate admitting you hate your current job

Ok, fine. So you hate your current job. Sorry/not sorry. So, what now? Do you go kicking and screaming to a recruiter? Jump into the world of freelance? Start your own shop? It all depends on your goals and your savings account. At least now you know where your head's at and you can turn your creative focus from that brief you hate, into finding a new job you love. Look for somewhere that will help you re-light the fire. Don't let your current job keep you from loving your career. Once you admit it is time to move on, that's exciting.

Give yourself the chance to love advertising again. To see your job as Pancho González, CCO/Founder, Inbrax does.

> Do it with pleasure, with love, and turn that not just into something that gives you the chance to pay your accounts, your bills, but something that helps you to build a strong path for next generations, and to inspire people. I've been this business for 30 years and (I feel like), I don't work in advertising. Advertising is my hobby.

Chapter 6

How not to hate your portfolio

I'll never forget the day I lost my portfolio. I was standing at baggage claim at LaGuardia airport late on a Monday night in 2003, waiting for my portfolio to show up on the carousel after a marathon day of interviews for a copywriter position at The Hiebing Group (now simply, Hiebing) in Madison, WI. This was the first year I moved to New York City, and still hadn't landed an advertising job. I'd gotten a little desperate, maybe a little homesick, and took a call from a recruiter about a gig that would take me back to the Midwest. I figured, "What have I got to lose?" Turns out, my portfolio was the answer, because it never showed up. You might be thinking "What do you mean your portfolio? Isn't that just a collection of links on your website." Yes, that's true now. But this was back when creatives actually printed physical portfolio pieces and mounted them on super black 100 presentation boards using (probably toxic) mounting spray.

You would spend HUNDREDS of dollars on the mounting supplies, cut the boards to size yourself, then go to Kinkos and spend HUNDREDS MORE printing each ad (yes, just a portfolio of print ads). Once you had your huge, heavy stack of proof you could write an ad, you had to buy a gigantic portfolio case to carry them around in. I think mine cost around $250 and I loved it so much. It was a 2-ft. × 3-ft. black, hard shell, vinyl-coated case. I think there may have even been a lock on it.

Future advertising rock star coming through!

I felt like a serious badass striding around with that thing in hand, like how a rock star oozes cool just by carrying a guitar case. *Out of the way! Future advertising rock star coming through!* That is, until my portfolio case disappeared forever. I have this fantasy in my head that whoever wound up finding it (or stole it?), used it to get a job and is out there somewhere living a parallel advertising career. Like the 1998 movie *Sliding Doors*, but instead of Gwenyth Paltrow missing her train, it's me missing my portfolio.

DOI: 10.4324/9781032615707-6

On top of all the printing and mounting costs, back in the day, you also had to make what was called a "mini book" – a much smaller, more portable, often 8.5" × 11" in horizontal orientation, leave-behind of your portfolio. That was another day at Kinkos, printing off hundreds of full-color pages, punching holes down the spine, and then hand-binding each of them INDIVIDUALLY. Printing off stickers with your name and contact info for the cover, and then hoping the creatives you share it with don't just toss it in the garbage trash can..

It was a hard-shell life, for us

So, from that fateful day, when my badass, rock star, hard-shell portfolio case never arrived at the baggage carousel, it was all mini books for me. But that didn't last long either, as basically overnight, every creative was expected to have a website (usually on cargocollective.com) and from there, the level of craft has risen beyond anything a hard-shell case could ever contain.

Of course, this is not a chapter about your portfolio as a printed stack of blackboards, but as the old famous BBDO slogan said, it's about *THE WORK. THE WORK. THE WORK.* It's about making a statement about the kind of creative you are via the work you're most proud of. You probably already know most of what follows, but a reminder never hurts. So repeat after me, as we recite the Portfolio Creed:

This is my portfolio! There are many like it, but this one is mine!

Your portfolio. Your book. Your site. Whatever you call it, it's the one thing in this business that is 100% completely yours. You can do whatever you want. There is no right or wrong way to do it. In the spirit of this book, what follows is a how-not-to guide, based on the following principles.

1 Order matters.
2 All killer, no filler. Every piece is a statement.
3 Side projects are mandatory.
4 Don't hide your awards.
5 An archive, yes. A dumping ground, no.
6 Eventually, you may not need a portfolio.

Order matters: how not to organize your site

Unlike a presentation to clients and the different philosophies on where to put the recommended idea (first? last?), in your portfolio – your best, most famous, most well-known, biggest, and boldest expression of who you are as a creative MUST COME FIRST. Simple as that. Don't bury it. Don't hide it. Put it at the top. Even if it's a few years old, if it's your best – or if it won you an Emmy, or a Grand Prix – it belongs at the top of the podium.

From there, the order of the remaining work can be debated, but the importance of quality cannot. Don't put anything on your site, especially in the first 5–7 slots, that isn't amazing. Lead with incredible, follow with amazing, then super awesome, and so on.

Don't put new work near the top because it's new. You may be tired of looking at your work and think your site needs a refresh, but resist that urge. If it's new work that is also amazing, then go for it, but don't post it just because it's new and you're bored. If it's not standout, take it out.

All killer, no filler: how not to include anything so-so

For the Sum 41 fans reading this, no, that was not a reference to their debut album. I was more of a fan of The Strokes. This is the phrase you need ringing in your head when picking out what gets featured on your site. All killer work, no filler work. Everything needs to be amazing, and have a reason for being featured. A killer TVC. A killer stunt. A killer branded content series. A killer side project. A killer social campaign. Be brutal. Kill weaklings. Or put them in an archive tab. Just not on the front page.

The pieces you feature send a message to recruiters and creative leaders about the kind of work you'll create going forward. It's also a test of your eye for great work. Don't include the so-so stuff or you'll leave them with a so-so feeling. If it won an award, it's killer. If it won a bunch of awards, it's definitely killer. If it didn't bring home any hardware, it can still be killer.

When I look at portfolios, I often look at the first two or three pieces. Then, I scroll down to the bottom and look at the last one. Then I randomly pick one or two from the middle. Then I look at where the creative worked. I know this blows up the previous section on order, but not really. You still need to lead with your absolute best work, and then think about the overall story you want all the work to tell. But don't include anything weak, even near the bottom, because it will get seen.

How not to be just another ad person? Have a side project/hustle

It used to be that all you needed to do to get a job in advertising was a portfolio filled with great ads. Makes sense, right? You wanna make ads? Show us you can make ads. Then, there was a shift. It wasn't enough to just be good at ads anymore. You also had to prove your creativity outside of work, too with a side project. If real projects got you noticed. Side projects got you remembered.

I will admit, half the people who ask about the work on my site, reference my side projects as much as my agency work, maybe more. Why? Because they are a pure creative expression. No clients. No briefs. No notes, please. A side project is your thing. And it's a thing you need to have today to be taken seriously. But relax. You're creative. You'll think of something.

So how do you find a side project? You don't. A side project finds you. Believe me, I've tried to sit down and force myself to think of my next creative project and nothing comes out. Inspiration is a real thing, and you can't force it. Like when I decided to start a music blog back in 2009. I didn't know what form it would take, I just wanted to write one. I loved indie rock but didn't want to just create a derivative Pitchfork. I was at WKNY at the time, working late with a partner on some ESPN project probably, when I blurted out "What if I called it 100 Bands in 100 Days? I could go see live music for 100 days straight and write about it." Eric Stevens, my partner at the time, said "You could do that." And that was it. The idea was born (Figure 6.1).

I didn't know *100 Bands in 100 Days* would become a pivotal creative moment for me, and a minor cultural moment that got picked up in the national press and eventually became a short documentary that would hit the festival circuit, including South by Southwest (SXSW) where it was nominated for the Grand Jury Award. I just had a moment of inspiration and ran with it. Since completing it, I would hear other creatives say they used it as inspiration in presentations to clients, which was weird to hear. Talk about full circle.

Cut to five years later, when my father-in-law filed the IRS paperwork to start the Woodstock Comedy Festival LLC, and suddenly, I had my next creative side project as CD and co-producer. That one lasted five years, and wasn't even my idea. But I couldn't miss the opportunity (Figure 6.2).

Smash cut to today, as I bang away at my MacBook keyboard for this book. Another side project that found its way into my orbit. Not by luck, but not on purpose either. I pitched a book idea to an editor simply because I couldn't think of a good reason not to. I'd always wanted to write a book, just didn't know what kind. And here we are.

But that's just me. There are so many more worth mentioning. Kurt Lenard started a furniture company called 31 and Change. Julie Rutigliano created the hilarious Instagram account Everythangsgreat. Lisa Preston is a photographer. Camilo Ruano is an insanely talented illustrator. Anjali Rao does stand up. Rob Munk's an actor. And so on.

The point is creative side projects/side hustles are helpful for your sanity and for your career. But they are also elusive. Which is what makes them so rewarding, and also frustrating. If you hate the idea of having to not just be creative all day for work, but then also have a creative side project no one's paying you for, I get it. But, they're pretty much table stakes today.

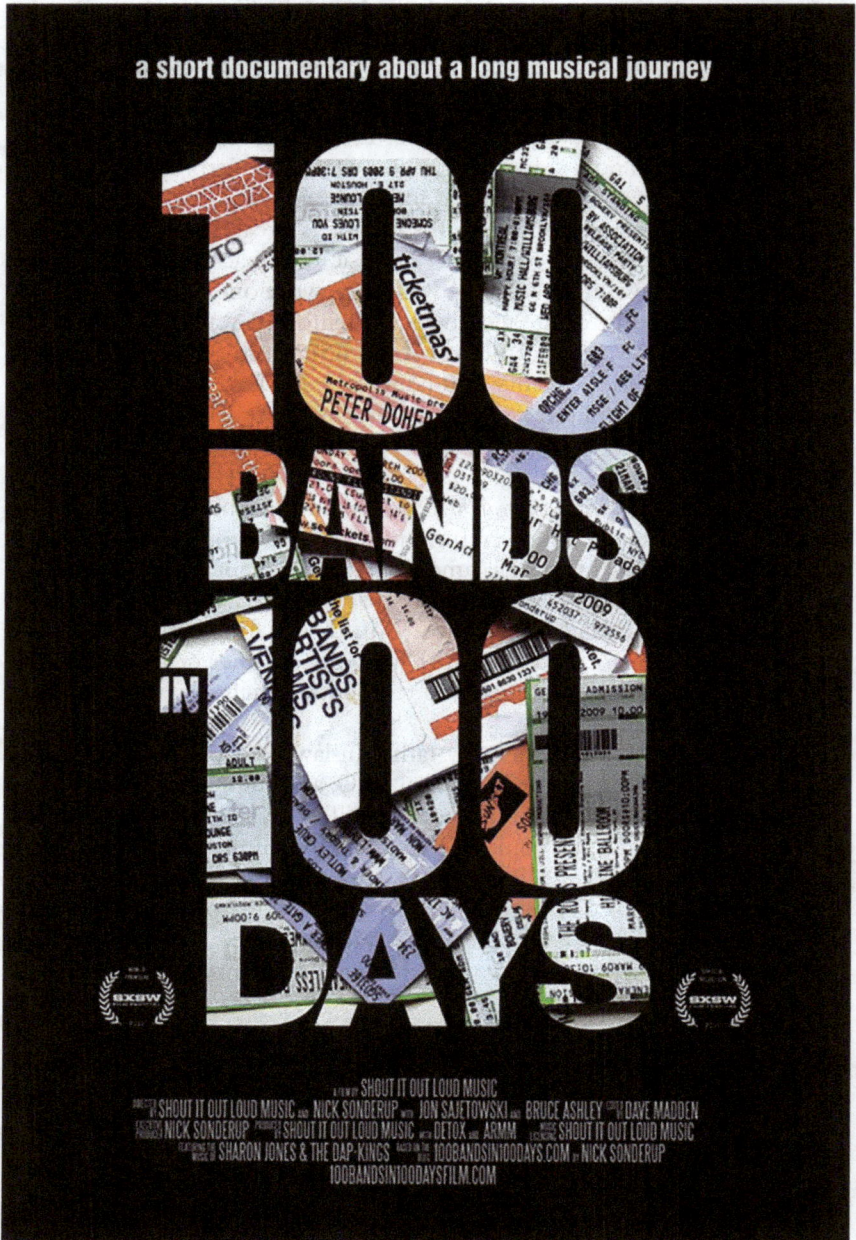

Figure 6.1 The *100 Bands in 100 Days* documentary debuted at the 2010 SXSW Film Festival. Poster design by Lance Rusoff. Courtesy of the author.

Figure 6.2 A side project like no other. The late Gilbert Gottfried headlined the 2017 Woodstock Comedy Festival. Photo by Justin Bettman.

They're also not the thing that will seal the deal for the job. Take it from Rory Hill (it's literally his job to know this stuff). "(A side project) won't get you ever the job on its own. I've never seen that." Ok, that's fair. But what it will do is give you a leg up if you have some great ads, and you're being compared to someone else who also has great ads. If you have a killer side project that shows another side of you – well, it certainly can't hurt.

How not to hate beating your chest about awards

If you don't beat your chest, no one will. Because that would be weird for someone else to walk up and start beating your chest. It's also probably assault. If you win awards, tell everyone. Not every day and not IRL. That would be really annoying and obnoxious. But do feature your awards prominently on your site. Listed in your bio, but also within the work that won the awards. They're not the only indication of talent, but awards do signal people to pay attention.

But, avoid the presentation of the awards getting in the way of the idea. Winning is validation of a great idea, but the idea itself still needs to be clear and stand on its own. Include the icon for the awards show somewhere on the page, like within the key image, or part of the description. If it won every single award in the world, congrats! But don't overshadow the idea with the plaudits. We still want to see the idea first and foremost. Get the logos or mentions in there, but not in the way.

How not to treat your site like an external hard drive

An archive is ok. A dumping ground is not. Your parents may hang onto every drawing you ever made or every test you took in high school. But your portfolio should not be the creative version of that. We covered what should go into the featured work on your site. We covered the side projects and awards that should also play a prominent role in your portfolio. When it comes to other work you've made throughout your career, it's okay to have an "Archive" section, so long as it doesn't just become the place where you put every single thing you've ever done. All work still needs to be great, and have a reason for being there, whether to show a specific capability (digital, social, stunts) or a range of brand categories.

Approach an archive strategically, not emotionally. Putting too much work in the archive runs the risk of undoing the care and craft of the previous points. If you aren't sure, create the pages and then hide them on your site. Turn them on if an agency asks for specific category or executional samples. Just don't turn them all on, all at the same time.

How not to hate eternally updating your site

Who knows? Maybe one day you won't need a portfolio. It doesn't happen to many, but it can happen. You reach a point in your career that your name and creative reputation replace any need for you to log into Squarespace and update your "recent work" section. Your title and agency are enough. Just Google your heroes right now. They probably don't have a site. They have a LinkedIn page or a page on The One Club and other awards shows. You'll see interviews, thought pieces, PR headlines, and probably a bio page on the agency website they founded or rose the ranks within. Or they have their own agency, and that's enough of a portfolio.

But, according to Rory Hill, "That's pretty uncommon. Let's use a soccer analogy. That's like a top Premiere League player who's being bought on their earned reputation. Most people have to be scouted." For all of you "scouted" out there, you still need either something (a site) that shows off your work or to be so amazing at networking, that you can just walk into a freelance job based on your reputation and past work. If you're there, good on you. If you're still updating a site, choose wisely. While reciting the Portfolio Creed of course...

This is my portfolio! There are many like it, but this one is mine!

Chapter 7

How not to hate going freelance

Is freelance just a fancy word for unemployed? Sometimes, yes. Sometimes, no. It depends on how frequently the jobs are coming in, your current mental health, and frankly, how committed you are to making it a lifestyle. For me, freelance could feel like FUNemployment one day, and the exact opposite the next. It took me years in the business to give it an honest try and for the year I was on the freelance market, it was one of the hardest.

On one hand, I was able to go skiing in Vermont on a Wednesday afternoon, then work on a screenplay the next day in a friend's cabin in the woods. Those days were amazing. But then there were other days filled with stop/start outreach on briefs that came and went. "We're filling it internally," was the usual response. And the briefs that started and ended early, pitches that weren't won and didn't turn into longer-term contracts. The feast and famine really harshed my freelance vibe, bro.

Figure 7.1 Eric Stevens. CD, Art Director, Writer.

The freedom was great, the uncertainty was not. Or maybe that was just my experience? But it could be yours, too. Best to be prepared yourself so the panic doesn't set in. If it does, hopefully this chapter will help.

Follow me to freelance freedom

Eric Stevens (TBWA Chiat/Day, CAA, W+K), freelance CD, has been a freelancer for over ten years. At first, he says it was a leap of faith. But ultimately, he doesn't ever see going back.

When you quit the full-time advertising race you get a broader perspective of the industry as a whole. It becomes

DOI: 10.4324/9781032615707-7

less about chasing that awesome brief or prestigious title and more about selling yourself as an authority in the space and delivering on the assignment. You learn new skills. And I think the business part of it all is just as interesting as the creative part.

Eric's point about seeing the business from another perspective is a sentiment I heard a lot. So is the idea of control, which Josh Dimarcantonio (Zambezi, Deutsch, CAA, TBWA Chiat/Day, W+K), another long-time freelancer, addressed.

Figure 7.2 Josh Dimarcantonio. ECD, Writer.

> For a lot of people, freelance feels scary, chaotic, unpredictable. For me, it's about one word: control. Control over how hard you work, how often you work, how you choose to work. For over a decade and a half, I was salaried at some of the best agencies in the world. And from inside those walls, freelance looked like walking a tightrope without a safety net. But once I jumped into it, I realized it's not instability—it's autonomy.

Autonomy one day, uncertainty the next. That's freelance in a nutshell. But Josh would tell you to keep the faith, "You don't always know when the next gig is coming. But trust me: it will come."

How not to hate the uncertainty of being freelance

1 Stockpile six months of savings before you jump. It takes a while to get people used to the idea of you being freelance and booking you. Then, it can take a while to get paid once they do.
2 Hit up all your friends at various agencies in positions of power.
3 Hit up all the internal recruiters you know. And those you don't.
4 Hit up former clients and offer to consult. Or be a sounding board.
5 Get a hobby. Ideally a creative one.
6 Go to ad parties and network. Yes, ad parties are back.
7 Go to movies. Hey. It's research!
8 Go to museums. It's also research.
9 Post on LinkedIn. Like, a lot.

How to not hate becoming one of those people who constantly posts on LinkedIn

This is a relatively new phenomenon for freelancers, but it's also very necessary. If you can stomach it, then the algorithm should reward you with the exposure you need to book gigs. You don't have to write a manifesto diatribe pontification every day. But you do need to decide on a cadence of content to engage with the platform so that you pop up in the feed of recruiters and agencies.

Pick a niche and become a "thought leader" in that field. Think: AI, design, or branded entertainment. Why the air quotes? Because are you really a thought leader just because you post a lot of thoughts? I'm not sure, says the guy writing a book no one asked for.

Comments and hashtags. Commenting on posts is an easy way to game the system. The algorithm takes over from there. Bonus points if your comments are funny or poignant. Hashtags may seem like old news, but it's another way to trick the algorithm.

Pre-write a bunch of posts. It will make the obligation feel less obligatory, and posting them feel less provoking.

Repost work you created that relates to a trending topic. You don't necessarily need new work if you can tie it to a current trend. Did LeBron just win the NBA Championship (again)? Post an ESPN or Nike spot you created with him. Boom! You're relevant!

Post videos. Why do you think people film podcasts? Because video still outperforms the written word on social media. Writing posts is better than nothing, but filming video is better than writing. You don't need a podcast to do it, but you do need to be comfortable filming yourself.

Best practices will continue to evolve, as the algorithms and AI get sharper and smarter. But for now, these basic tips should get your profile/face/voice, into the feed of more people who will reach out, when they have a brief you'd be great for.

How not to hate getting the freelance ball rolling

I asked Rory Hill, Executive Recruiter and Talent Director, for practical advice for anyone jumping into the freelance pool. What's the first thing you should do? What mistakes do people make? He had a lot of amazing insights to help, so I turned them into a list. Lists are fun, right? Right. So here's a list from Rory, rather than me blabbering on and on again…

Treat [going freelance] like getting a new job. You only have to give two weeks' notice at a job, right? So at the top of the month, reach out to your network, and tell them you're going freelance.

Line it up before you leave. Ideally, you have your first bit of freelance ready to go before you leave your current job.

Know the going rates. Gather enough information to know the current rates or at least ballparks. Are you at a $1,000 day rate? Or 1,500? Do a bit of work to understand the market.

Be willing to cut your price at the first gig. Just to get going and get your sea legs. Once you're much more in demand, then you can inflate your rate. You need to be constantly re-evaluating.

Get a good accountant. You need someone who can tell you whether you should be a w2 or an LLC or an S corp. Some agencies won't pay you if you're one over the other.

How not to hate not getting credit

The freedom of freelance can be amazing, we've established that. The flipside to that amazingness, however, is the lack of credit and final output you'll get for all the work you do. The freelance life isn't one of public praise, outside the agency you're working for. In rare cases, and unique agencies, freelancers can and do go on production. We do that a lot at StrawberryFrog.

We don't hide our freelancers from clients and often invite them on production if it makes sense for the project and budget. More often than not across the industry though, freelancers are a helping hand or a desperate lifeline. Outsiders. Mercenaries. Or, as Josh Dimarcantonio puts it, "You're a ghost creative – brought in, asked to quietly blow minds, then disappear." Dropping mics and moving on.

On the flip side of credit, while Jillian Goger (Mekanism, Droga5, McCann, Arnold), ECD/Writer, loves the detachment of freelance life, she also hates it.

> I find it extremely challenging to be detached. Having little to no influence about the direction of the brand. Having little to no interaction with the client. Most of the brands I work on I really grow to care about. And it's hard to let go.

Credit. Influence. What can you do about it as a freelancer? Not much, unfortunately. That doesn't mean you shouldn't tell agencies that you're available for a more engaged role, if they need. Like, being on the project through production. Or being in front of clients. It's good for them to know that you'd be committed enough to see it through. They may surprise you, and ask you to take a lower day rate in order to stretch it out over a period of time. Then, it's on you to decide if you want to be a ghost, or add to your book. Because that's the other reality of the fabulous freedom of freelance.

How not to hate your stale portfolio

You know that pressure you feel to keep refreshing your portfolio when you're on staff. When you're a freelancer, the pressure can feel extra heavy. And it's not just you, the people looking for talent see it, too. "Books can get stale," says Rory Hill. "Somewhere in the three to five-year mark, your portfolio can lose its luster. You're reaching out to hiring managers with the same book that they saw when you first came out." Oof. That's a reality check. Some freelancers take a full-time job, just to update their book. Then jump back to freelance once it feels fresh. Others make it clear that they worked on a campaign for this or that, but as a freelancer so obviously their name wasn't on it. Others, just keep riding the fame from their previous work.

How not to hate chasing people for payment or negotiating your rate

There is no way. That part is not fun. Simple as that. But once you do get paid...

How not to hate doing it for the money

When freelance pays off. It can really pay off. For Eric Stevens, that's the point. "To me this is a more transactional business than many make it out to be. So, all I ask from it in return for my time is money." And if that's your goal, that's fine. Barry Manilow sold State Farm their famous "Like a Good Neighbor, State Farm is There" jingle for $500 back in the '70s.[1] Today, selling ideas can make you a lot more than that. Josh Dimarcantonio would know. He's been in the freelance world for years now.

> Once you establish a network of people you like to work for—and who like you back—the financial upside of freelance is hard to beat. Start your own LLC, hire the right accountant, and you'll be shocked how lucrative coming up with "silly little ideas" can get.

In other words, silly ideas may not be so silly, once you realize how much they're actually worth.

Freelance can be a rough ride, or it can be a smooth sailing on the Riviera on your new schooner. If you ever make the choice to dive in, or are forced into the deep end, know that it's about the same thing the rest of the business is about – great ideas, strong relationships, and never mailing it in. At the end of the day, this business runs on ideas. Those who continue to crank out the great ones, whether on staff or on contract, will find themselves with more briefs, more work, and less things to hate.

Note

1 "'Stuck on Band-Aid' and Other Unforgettable Jingles You Probably Didn't Know Barry Manilow Created". Kate Hogan. *People Magazine*, March 4, 2023.

Chapter 8

How not to hate the way we work now

There used to be this place we used to have to go every day. It was called the office. Imagine that. If you can remember those days, odds are you miss the good parts, like free leftover pizza in the conference room or intense foosball tournaments. Or, you might remember the stupid games you would create when you should've been working on a brief, like Shelf Ball or Pipe Ball, both invented at WK+NY during my time. Shelf Ball went on to become an actual TV spot as part of ESPN's "Without Sports…" campaign (Google it). Or you may miss seeing a campaign tacked up on big blackboards. You probably don't miss being at the office until 5 am the night before a pitch, but at least you weren't alone. The office was more than a place you went. It was part of the job. Now, as we question the role of an office, we're also questioning how we behave as creatives.

We're questioning productivity: are we more productive at home? We're questioning teamwork: should we go in to mentor the juniors? We're questioning spontaneity: can random moments of inspiration happen at home? We're even questioning the space itself. Do we need an actual office, or could we just meet at a co-working space, coffee shop, or library? These are all good questions and we have a lot of good opinions.

But I am not an expert on the future of work, so don't expect what follows to be an exhaustive psychological or financial analysis. Expect a bunch of opinions from a bunch of people like you and me. In the end, only you can figure out how much you do or don't hate the idea of going to the office. Whether you have a choice in it, or not.

Don't call it a comeback (because it's partial)

I don't think you need to be in an office to do great work, but you can't just sit home in your pajamas all day long.
—Scott Goodson, CEO/Founder, StrawberryFrog

DOI: 10.4324/9781032615707-8

During the pandemic, many agencies hired fully remote employees, or let employees move anywhere in the country. The thinking went, if we're working from home anyways, we should be hiring and retaining the best talent, regardless of location. That type of policy is largely over, not just for the big Publicis of the world, but for indies too, like StrawberryFrog, Pereira O'Dell, and Mother are also requiring employees to be close enough to the office to be able to pop in at a moment's notice. Makes sense though, right? If clients want to meet in person, they expect their agency partners to be nearby. It is a service business, after all. But not all agencies are being as prohibitive. Some agencies, like Arts & Letters in Richmond, VA still hire employees across the country, which is a bit of a no brainer. As someone who's recently been on both ends

Figure 8.1 Scott Goodson. CEO/ Co-Founder of StrawberryFrog.

of the hiring spectrum – staff and freelance – Kurt Lenard (Digitas, BBDO, W+K), GCD/Art Director agrees, "Hybrid opens the door to talent. No longer is there east coast talent or west coast talent. It opens doors for both creatives and agencies to work with the best, and if not the best, something new and different."

Essentially, there's still no one size fits all for agencies. Just one size fits many. It's all about finding the right equation. Hybrid work takes the right people with the right attitude, the right mentality, and the right culture to make it work, according to Lenard. "If your equation is off and you have folks who hide behind slack chats, if you hire folks who find it difficult to engage in work or culture or find folks who lack responsibility, it simply won't work."

For me, when the company Zoom called its employees back to the office in the fall of 2023,[1] that's when I knew the pajama party was over. Today, we're hovering somewhere between a hybrid world and a full Return to Office (RTO). If you're still fully remote while reading this, consider yourself lucky. For the rest of us, the perfect answer is still a mystery and probably always will be. Even Cornell University[2] smarties can't figure out:

Some data shows that work-from-home (WFH) employees express higher levels of satisfaction, improved well-being, and increased engagement. Studies also found that workers can experience more stress resulting in higher turnover. Yet research often fails to differentiate between various types of work-from-home employees.

Wow! What a convincing stance. Anything else, Cornell?

Remote workers are more engaged than their on-site counterparts. But longer hours, job pressure, and blurred work-life roles can skew the benefits.

And that's only one source. There are so many more. You've probably read them, re-posted them, or wrote a long LinkedIn post about them. But what do they know? Those studies aren't about you. And only you know how you're most productive. Plus, who even cares about studies, or data, or research results?! We work in advertising! Oh wait...

Questioning productivity: Where are we most productive?

Creatives and the powers that be are going to differ wildly on this question, mainly because creatives have always felt more productive outside the office. This is not a new phenomenon. It's why many creatives prefer to WFH or at a coffee shop. I think the conflicted summation from Jillian Goger, ECD/Writer, kinda sums it up for me. And for many others I've spoken to.

I hate that working in the office is infinitely more productive and, ultimately, way more rewarding. It's so cliche but there's no substitution for a writer's room. Mentoring over zoom is just not a thing. Teamwork can happen remotely but it's way more effective face-to-face. And I truly, full-throatedly hate that I love being in person.

When *Adweek* reported on the 2025 memo announcing WPP's new RTO policy, in which WPP CEO Mark Read said, "From the beginning of April this year, the expectation...will be that most of us spend an average of four days a week in the office...we do our best work when we are together in person."[3] I'm pretty sure a collective creative groan was detected on the Richter scale.

Productivity is a hard thing to quantify and even harder to find a unifying position on. For creatives, productivity might mean quiet stretches of time to work and create. For non-creatives, it might mean more butts in seats and more client meetings in the agency. You basically need to think about your personal KPIs, in this case, Key Productivity Indicators. When do you want to be "creatively productive" vs. "agency productive"? Because they are very different things. One gets you a great creative product, the other gets you a team finishing each other's sentences in a pitch. Both are super important, but neither can claim dominance.

How not to hate being told when and where to be productive

It's a mindset shift, really. Ask yourself, is this a "creatively productive" day? Or is this an "agency productive" day? Then obviously, do what works best for you. If you've got a lot of writing or design to get done, you can get up early and knock it out before the day starts, or before leaving for the office. Or you can block your calendar for chunks at a time, regardless of your location, and ignore everything else. Or you can work late when there's no one around to bug you. Yes, these are all the obvious ways, but the question above is the most important part.

When I found productivity difficult working on this book, I asked myself when I could commit time to finish it, then blocked off 9 am–12 pm every Saturday until my deadline. Suddenly, I started hating my deadlines less. I scheduled my creative productivity, and it mostly worked.

The "agency productive" days are harder. You will need to do all of the above prep work to fit in the creativity, but it will be worth it. The teamwork, chemistry, and unknown gained from being together won't take away from the end creative product, they will enhance it.

Questioning teamwork: do we have to be together to be a team?

When I asked Lisa Preston (The New School, The Today Show, MTV), a VP of marketing and 30+ year veteran on both the agency and client side, her thoughts on our current hybrid work culture, she didn't mince words. "I hate, hate, hate working remotely. Marketing is communal." She voiced the pain many people feel about every conversation being a scheduled thing in a WFH environment. It's the difference between blurting out an idea to a colleague vs. having to check someone's schedule and set up a Zoom if you have a random thought. Or decide whether to send them an email, slack, or text. On one hand, Lisa's addressing the spontaneity issue in a hybrid world. But she's also talking about what it means to work as a team.

Figure 8.2 Lisa Preston. VP of Marketing.

Lisa helped me get my first job at MTV by standing up, walking down the hallway, and dropping my portfolio on the desk of Jeffrey Keyton, SVP/Head of Design at MTV in 2003. Would that happen today? Sure. People recommend others all the time. But less people stand up, walk over, and say, "You should really check out this guy's portfolio" followed by "Did you hear what happened at the MTV2 party last night?" Partially because MTV2 probably isn't throwing many parties anymore, and mostly because of the whole office thing. So I do agree with Lisa when she said, "It's just not the same." But I'm not sure the "same" is ever coming back, and that's not a bad thing.

Listen, I've pitched and won business entirely on Zoom, with all of my colleagues and clients never being in the same room together. I had to. We all did, out of pure survival. I've also hired a junior creative who started his first day, at his very first full-time job, from his basement. I've even hired an AD who I never actually met in the flesh because he quit before ever coming back to an office. I'm sure you have, too. Those were weird times, for many reasons. But today, the same question remains: Do we have to be together to work together as a team?

How not to hate taking one for the team

I believe the children are our future, teach them...and, you know the rest. But the children in this case are the juniors, not just creatives, but across all departments. Think of them when you're complaining about having to go in on a Wednesday. Also, remember that you're lucky to be in a creative field with flexibility. We're not ER surgeons or garbage collectors, who would absolutely roll their eyes if they heard us whining about being forced back to the office.

Is it the responsibility of all non-junior creatives to teach the next generation of creatives? Not just the CDs. All of us. Now more than ever, because of how little time they spend soaking in the intangibles. It's not just about briefings, or creative check-ins, or going out to lunch. It's about something more.

Rory Hill gave it to me straight, once again.

Some of those great relationships between a CD and a team are because of you went through the fire and they really saw your mettle, and they want to invest in you, because they go 'That person didn't let me down when I stayed till four in the morning they did too, when I asked them to come in an extra day, even though they were sick, they did whatever.' Some of that gets lost, and then some of how to behave also gets lost.

Remember: with great flexibility comes great responsibility. The juniors need you/us. They don't know what they don't know so while they may complain about having to be in the office three days a week, the knowledge they gain is not something they can learn through Zoom or Teams. Go in, and teach them the Dos and Don'ts of working together, in the flesh. Do make eye contact. Do read non-verbal cues. Do kick someone out of the conference room because you booked it. Don't bring your laptop to a meeting, unless you're presenting. Don't open a new browser tab in the middle of a meeting and check the weather. Don't grab a quick salad by yourself, but ask someone to go with you instead.

Not just for the juniors. Everyone deserves your attention. When you're in the office, there's a thing happening called chemistry. You need to be building it, fostering it, watering it like a Chia Pet. Because when you do find yourself in a pitch meeting on Zoom, if the bond is built it will be felt, and the pitch will be yours. And no one hates winning.

Questioning spontaneity: can in-the-moment inspiration happen at home?

Today, we're all working in some hybrid form, and that life comes with a lot of freedom. Some days it can feel like you're getting paid to watch TV, dust your living room, or go grocery shopping. I'm guessing those aren't the reasons you got into this business, save for the watching TV part. Other days you can feel like a prisoner in your own home, glued to Zoom all day, or writing tirelessly from your couch until you realize you haven't moved in six hours and your neck is as stiff as a Board presentation.

But these are all the tangible elements of hybrid work. What about the intangibles? The spontaneous moments you can't plan on or manufacture? What are we missing out on, by not being around each other every day? Is creative taking a hit? Or just evolving?

Ask ten creatives in advertising and you'll get 30 opinions. And probably some recommendations on the best new TV shows or indie rock albums to check out. But I digress. It's hard to argue that by not being around each other more, we're missing out on some of the spontaneity necessary in a creative field. That doesn't mean we're less creative than we used to be. We're differently creative.

How not to hate not knowing the next thing out of your mouth

Some bemoan the loss of spontaneity with less in-person office days. I'm gonna be contrarian say, I think the opposite is true. Today, anytime you have a thought, you have a bazillion ways to share it with someone, in the moment – text, audio text, Slack, Gchat, Teams, email, Whatsapp…and yes, even a phone call. The fact that we're so overly connected today and less conditioned to hold back sharing whatever is on our mind – the result is more spontaneous ideation. Just because we're not "in the office" doesn't mean we're not working. A creative mind never stops. So while hallway conversations may not happen as often, that doesn't mean less in the moment. Speaking of the agency hallway...

Questioning the space itself: do we need an actual office?

> I wouldn't say I've been missing it, Bob.
> —Peter Gibbons (played by Ron Livingston), from *Office Space*

A 2023 State of Remote Work study found that "98% of respondents would like to work remotely, at least some of the time, for the rest of their careers." The study says that's up from 97% in the same study the previous year.[4] WFH FTW basically. It's not going anywhere, but do we need an actual office to go to? Or could we just all meet at a co-working space? Or a coffee shop? Or a library? Business owners have been pondering these questions ever since 2020, and haven't found any silver bullet answer.

Scott Goodson, CEO/Co-founder of StrawberryFrog wasn't so sure,

> When COVID hit, I was like, let's get rid of the office. We don't need an office. I thought this was a big moment, but there was a big push to have an office. I just think, you know, humans have an ability to interact with each other, and after a while, what initially feels odd becomes normal.

Agencies have tried all kinds of different ways to lure people back, like free lunches, happy hours, and parties. I've even heard of agencies threatening termination if employees don't return. For these agencies, the actual office is clearly the answer. It would be hard to fire someone for not showing up at the local Starbucks four days a week.

I agree and believe an office of some kind is still the best answer. I think people still want a consistent, communal place to go. Does it have to look like or behave like a traditional office? No. But picking a different coffee shop each day, or subscribing to a co-working space that will never feel ownable, isn't the answer either.

How not to hate the actual office space your agency is making you go to

Most of the creatives I talked to miss the office to some degree. Well, except for one CD who when I asked what if anything she missed about the office, said: "Nothing. I hate all offices." I can't imagine how naming her would help her career, so left it out. For the rest of us who are being asked, strongly encouraged, or forced to return to an office, the upside is other people will be there.

Sure, you see plenty of people on Zoom or Teams or whatever. Too many people, all at once. Little people in little boxes in their little coat closets, apologizing for the jackhammer outside their window or cat walking across their keyboard. But those 2" × 1" people are somehow not even completely real, even if we know they really exist. Why? Because we're never actually looking anyone in the eyes, just a screen with a human-looking person digitally reconstructed and spit back to us in a flat screen collection of pixels. And all this not looking people in the eye really hurts your eyes at the end of the day. You know what would help that?

Go to the office more. And stay at the office less

If your in-office day is Wednesday, go on a Tuesday also. Or a Thursday. Or both. The change of scenery helps. So does being at an actual office desk, with an expensive office chair and an overpriced chopped salad. Invite one or two colleagues you're working with on a project to join you. Grab a drink after. Or better yet, during the day.

Just because you go to the office, doesn't mean you have to stay all day. Depending on where you live, this may not be helpful, but if you can pull off the morning in the office, and then head home for your afternoon meetings. Or duck out early and go to a museum, or lunch with a vendor, or meet up with other creative minds. It will make you hate the office less if you're there more, and then leave early.

Ban laptops from in-person meeting

I know this seems insane now, but there were days when the only person who brought a laptop to a meeting was the 20-something social media Community Manager. Now it's all of us. If you can, keep computers out of meetings. You'll find something really amazing happens. You listen. Then other people listen. You make decisions. You get stuff done. You don't multi-task. You solo task.

Turn the office into a comedy club

Organize a comedy night at the office. Or a poker game. Or a poetry slam. Bring back the weirdness. It's too easy to just treat the office as a different place to Zoom from. Play hide and seek. Order a singing telegram. Blast Norwegian Black Metal in the kitchen. I don't care what you do, just make it memorable. Then challenge someone else – publicly, over an all-agency email – to make next week even weirder.

Scott Goodson, CEO/Co-Founder of StrawberryFrog, remains excited about the evolution of how we work.

I'm open to new and better ways of working. I'm naturally open to new and better because that's always been kind of what I believe it's one of the reasons why I think StrawberryFrog is still standing. Being willing to change and do things differently and be open to a new way of thinking. I'm not tied to dogma.

Using the new tools in your toolbox

Freelancers. Permalancers. Contractors. Fractionals. Whatever you want to call them, the way we work today relies, not depends, on gig workers. This is not a new phenomenon but has definitely taken on a different shape recently. As agencies strive to do more with less, the gig worker isn't something you can really afford to hate. They have a place at the table. And if you treat them right, they will contribute to that agency's culture the same way an FTE can.

Invite them to the party, literally

Put freelancers on the same agency invites you would send to a permanent employee. Let them present their ideas, in front of clients, if that's cool with management and clear to all parties involved. If you can afford to invite them to the shoot. And the post. And the holiday party. Why not? A decade ago this would've seemed crazy. But today, it's how we work.

I learned all of this from working at StrawberryFrog which has always had a deep bench of freelancers/permalancers. What used to be novel is the new normal. Embrace it.

"For years, people who used freelancers didn't talk about them. They were hidden in the back. But I would put them front and center," said Scott Goodson. The agency's philosophy is to treat freelancers like FTEs, not mercenaries. Don't let them hide in the shadows, bring them to the party – literally.

Don't hate. Incorporate

Work the gig workers into your staff plan, your weekly status calls, and your company culture. You'll all be better off for it. Bring in the right someone, not just someone who can write. Need huge, platform thinking? There's a freelance team for that. Need activations? Stunts? Amazing OOH. A brand book? A design template? A new logo?

There's more talent at your fingertips than ever before, waiting to jump on your project.

Pay them fair and they won't stray far. Be upfront about what you have, and reasonable about what you can expect. If you can't pay a freelancer their usual rate, agree on a length of project, or percentage of their day. Everyone wants to work, but no one wants to get screwed. On both sides.

The new not normal

It's been four years and I still screw up sharing on Zoom sometimes. Or I forget them that I'm on mute, or off camera. That's because this is not a natural way to work. But, it is how we will always work from here on out. So get over it. Oh, you hate Teams? Guess what, so do your clients. Let's chit-chat about something other than how annoying said platform is while we wait for everyone to join, ok? Thanks.

With collaborative, sharing apps like Google Docs, Figma, Miro, and others, why do we even have Microsoft Word anymore? I guess for the same reason we still have paper and pens. They have a place, just not for everyone. My kids build Google slide decks for their Christmas lists that are filled with sleek transitions, music, and GIFs. At age 12, their pathway to working in advertising is almost certainly set. We professionals have no excuse for not mastering these apps.

Today, we can go from a germ of an idea with no presentation deck one day, to a pro deck ready for a CMO Zoom overnight. You can throw together an idea, share it with a freelance team in Europe, so they work while you're asleep and wake up to something amazing. Then polish it together in real time while they sip on a cafe con leche in Barcelona, and you crush a BEC in Brooklyn. This isn't "new" anymore, but when you take a step back and think about how long it would take to develop an idea even five years ago, it's mind-blowing. Add the newest tools in your toolbox, like ChatGPT, Midjourney, and other AI or LLM tools to the mix and there's a whole lot to not hate about how we work today (see Chapter 9 for more on this).

The new expectations

With faster tools comes the expectation of warp-speed creativity. It's true that we can build amazing things in record time. Clients expect it, and we expect it of ourselves. It's exciting and maddening. On the flip side, our job is to keep things in perspective and keep the expectations manageable. Protect the time we need, even within the hyperspeed we now work. Ideas still need to be nurtured. Run, but don't rush. Don't skip a step (see Chapter 2).

Don't put sexy over breakthrough. Don't polish a turd. You'll always regret it. And clients will lose faith.

Just because we can multi-task like never before, doesn't mean we should do it all day, everyday. Having casting callbacks up on an iPad while you're simultaneously in a Zoom meeting on your laptop that you're ignoring while you put the finishing touches on another idea in a Google slides deck may seem wildly productive. But you're giving 30% to each instead of 100% to any. Stop it. Tell account, or production, or clients you need to focus on one or the other. Set an expectation of greatness not doneness, before you get to the point where what you're making is full of dullness. And you hate it because you can't give any of it the attention it needs.

The only way to really not hate the way we work today is to figure out how to make this entire chapter work for you.

Notes

1 "Zoom, Other Remote-Work Champions Call Employees Back to the Office". Chip Cutter. *The Wall Street Journal*. August 8, 2023.
2 "What Science Says about the Pros and Cons of WFH". Jessica Elliott. *CO by U.S. Chamber of Commerce*. February 22, 2023.
3 "Publicis Asks U.S. Employees to Come in Three Days a Week". Kyle O'Brien. *Adweek*. August 7, 2023.
4 "State of Remote Work 2023". *Buffer.com*. April 4, 2024.

Chapter 9

How not to hate the shiny new object

Before I started to write this book, I kinda hated Artificial Intelligence (AI), save for the kind that's always been in video games. Skepticism is necessary and valuable when it comes to new tech, and it's especially true when it comes to the world-changing tech of AI More than any other before it, we need to question AI like it's the lead suspect in a triple homicide, in an episode of *Law and Order*. Under the hot lights, handcuffed to a table, in the back of a dingy room at an undisclosed location. *Why did you murder so many creative careers? Where are the bodies? Have you no shame? There's no way you could've done this on your own. WHO ARE YOU WORKING FOR?!!*

When I spoke to Jeff Kling, CCO/Founder of Das Favorite, he had a more, um, measured feeling toward AI, as he looked upwards toward the sky at whoever/whatever is listening. "I would just like to say that I really have deep respect and love for our AI overlords, and I just can't wait until they enslave us all in a hail of lasers." That doesn't sound like hate, right? It sounds like, um, complete and total, undying love, if you ask me (*wink*).

Oh, it ain't broke? Cool, let's fix it anyway

I think the real reason I used to hate AI was because I didn't see why it was necessary for creativity to head in this direction. Yes, it's easier to make storyboards and keyframes now, especially if you can't draw or aren't a Photoshop pro. If you're a writer like me, you would instead be pulling so-so stuff from Google images. Now I can go from having nothing to having an image of an octopus in a pinstriped suit, dealing blackjack on a rollercoaster in Central Park in less than a minute. The speed is undeniable. That image wasn't worth printing in this book though.

ADs like Camilo Ruano (Ogilvy, DDB, Pereira O'Dell) especially love it.

It saves me hours and hours of comps and photoshopping. The first time I used AI, we were asked by an ECD to make a whole storyboard for the

DOI: 10.4324/9781032615707-9

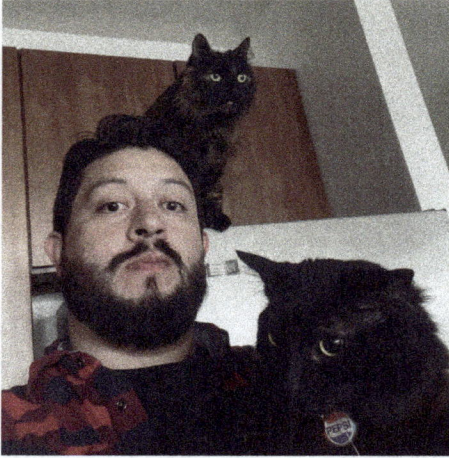

Figure 9.1 Camilo Ruano. CD, Art Director. Didn't create this in AI.

next day, starting at 4pm. In the old days, that would've meant no sleep. I solved it in one hour with AI.

But the speed wasn't enough to convince me. I couldn't understand *why* this technology was necessary.

Why would we want to create this world for ourselves? Where the craft isn't about making something from scratch with human hands, but instead of writing the right combination of words to spit out something created at incredible speed, but not really that unique or artful.

Ok, yes human hands have to do that too I guess. I was amazed by the output, but underwhelmed by how much everything looked like AI. Are we just going to create a whole new bank of stock imagery, but only made of AI? Is that the point?

Then it clicked. Trying to figure out the *Why would we bother?* isn't the point. It's the why not, and the how to. Or, in keeping with the theme of this book, the how not to. So here are the big questions this chapter will seek to answer.

1 **How not to hate feeling like you'll get left behind**
2 **How not to hate not knowing where this is all going**
3 **How not to hate AI being everywhere, all the time**

How not to hate feeling like you'll get left behind

I first started playing around with ChatGPT after reading *The New York Times* article "A Conversation With Bing's Chatbot Left Me Deeply Unsettled" by Kevin Roose. What started as innocently as my interaction above, soon took a sharp turn for Roose when, "At one point, it declared, out of nowhere, that it loved me. It then tried to convince me that I was unhappy in my marriage, and that I should leave my wife and be with it instead."[1] This was riveting stuff. The chatbot almost seemed sentient. Obviously, it wasn't. But this was my first wake-up call about the AI revolution headed our way like a runaway train. The prevailing feeling that followed wasn't one of fear or dread for humanity (that comes later), but something more personal – being left behind.

Scott Goodson, CEO/Founder, StrawberryFrog had a good way of putting it.

> We are moving into a period of what I call peacocks and ducks. There's going to be a lot of ducks swimming out there, but there are very few peacocks. I think a lot of ducks will lose their jobs. I think ducks will become irrelevant. So, don't be a duck. Be a peacock.

His point about the world we're entering raised a lot of questions for me, relating to advertising production for example.

Do we want to live in a world where we know and intentionally create work that no director directed, no actors auditioned for, no DP swapped lenses during, or no first AD yelled "roll sound"? A world where no script supervisor tracked all the takes, no stylist went shopping, no agency producer found the best place for dinner, where no creative got a green juice at 3 pm from craft services or no client had to leave the shoot early?

The thing about AI that made me feel better is that it still needs humans to make it great. Charles Aubert, Technology & Innovation Lead at Bluefish AI and a friend of mine, reminded me that AI can't come up with any new ideas, it can only create based on ideas humans have already had. Lisa Preston, a VP of Marketing, put it more bluntly,

> I don't believe machines are creative. You can feed it options. It can spit stuff out, but I don't think you're ever going to get the same capacity you get from a human. being generating ideas. It's all formulated from what it's been told, there's nothing original.

So, hey – score one for humans. That made me feel less like I was going to get enslaved by Skynet, or in a hail of lasers.

Humans will use AI going forward, no doubt. To what degree and what application is an open question. AI is the new shiny thing right now and for the foreseeable future. But it will not replace one thing that advertising has forever been built upon.

Storytelling still needs humans

Think of some of your favorite commercials. Mine are, "The Wind" by Epuron. Ikea "Lamp" by Crispin. Nike's "Write the Future" and "The High Life Man" by Wieden. Volkswagen "The Force" by Deutsch. These are some of the highest forms of storytelling in our business. And storytelling has always been and will continue to be created by humans. Scott Goodson agrees,

> Until such time as they put a metadata chip in our brain, and we don't have to think anymore, and our feelings will be completely controlled by machines then, storytelling is still the most important tool for us to engage other humans.

So how are we supposed to *not hate* the feeling, and the reality, that AI is moving so quickly that we might be left behind? First, you have to keep playing with it. Find the practical application that suits you and your team. You don't have to use every single creative application in order to stay current. But don't just sit on ChatGPT, either. Play around with different tools – image creation, video creation, music, voiceover. Have fun. Do it for yourself, not just your projects. Find solace in the fact that no one will have mastered all of it. And more importantly, no one will really know where it's headed.

Wherever it's going, Samira Ansari (Ogilvy, Deutsch, FCB), CCO/Art Director is optimistic that we will adjust.

> If COVID showed me anything, it was that we, as human beings, can adapt so quickly. AI is making us do that and is making some people uncomfortable. I love AI and what it can do for us. I love how it's making our lives easier.

How not to hate not knowing where this is all going

What if I told you we've already been doing the thing AI is doing as creatives? That's the point Steve Conner, CEO of Fluid Content, made when we got onto the subject. That kind of blew my mind a little, but also made me feel better. He said:

> When I first tried AI, I realize it's actually doing what we do and what we've trained ourselves to do for a living, because what we do is we take a corpus of data from whomever. We take all of this stuff together along with whatever they prepared for research, and then whatever the account person brought and we take all of that, and we use that to ruminate on and become something. That was our job as creatives, right?

Obviously, AI can do it a lot faster and with a lot more information. But I take his point. So if AI starts doing the bulk of our job for us, then what are we left to do? Ivan Rivera (Ogilvy, DDB, Pereira O'Dell) raised a point I've heard from a lot of creatives when he said that "the real fear is that we start becoming more editors than creators."

Josh Dimarcantonio (Zambezi, Deutsch, CAA, TBWA Chiat/Day, W+K) agrees and even predicts when it will happen. "In five years, our jobs will shift. We'll become curators. Editors. Directors. The line between 'creative director' and 'copywriter' will blur because everyone will be creatively collaborating with AI daily." But he also agrees that just because AI will become the norm, doesn't mean it will replace all of the creatives named Norm. "Will AI eventually take over the daily grind? Sure. Will it replace human creativity entirely? Never."

Figure 9.2 Ivan Rivera. CD, Writer.

It's widely accepted that there are seven basic narrative plots in storytelling and Shakespeare wrote them all. Humans have been rewriting these seven plots for over 400 years. Are we worried that AI is going to suddenly upend this and invent some new narrative that Shakespeare didn't? It won't. It can't. That doesn't mean it can't take these seven narrative plots and write seven different movies, novels, or comic books based on them. It definitely could, with the right prompts. Will we ask AI to do that? I for one don't want to hand this over to AI, when writing stories is the best part of what we do.

I contend that while creatives can at times lack proper motivation or inspiration, we are not lazy people. We have not become so bored of the creative process or hate what we do enough to want a computer to do it instead. That is, unless it conflicts with a yoga class, or Coachella. So the fact that creatives will just succumb to the ease and convenience of using AI to do all of their work is silly. If you picked up this book, you probably hate parts of the business, but if you've made it this far, you don't hate it enough to quit and become an organic goat farmer while AI tackles your Super Bowl brief.

Is that really where this is headed? Training AI tools so we don't need to come up with ideas anymore? Or even have a creative department that does it? In the wrong hands, possibly. But at the right shops, no way. Our love for the creative process and output is too strong (to say nothing of our egos).

In my conversation with Camilo Ruano, we agreed that the frustration that eventually leads to exhilaration when you finally crack a brief is the best part. "With AI, you don't have that frustration. You just have the idea." But that doesn't totally work for me, because the struggle is the fun part.

To Ivan Rivera's point earlier, being the editor of ideas, instead of the creator of them, is that where this is all headed? Will we all be CDs with AI as our creatives? Jeff Kling agreed that CDs aren't going anywhere, but he wasn't so sure about creatives. "AI doesn't replace the creative director or the agency. I believe an agency is only as strong or as powerful as its creative direction…so the rise of AI doesn't hurt the creative director, it hurts the creatives."

Will we replace human CWs and ADs with AI versions? Fully trained to create the kind of work we know we like, we know our clients will like, what our industry has awarded and in the style of what's most successful for any given category? Is that the future? I really hope not. Because if it is, where will groundbreaking ideas that surprise us because they don't do the above?

Camilo quoted Henry Ford when he said, "If I had asked people what they wanted, they would have said faster horses." It's debatable whether Ford actually said it, but the point is not. If we create ideas only based on what's worked before, we'll never create anything new.

Could we get the next "Hate something, change something." if we leave it up to AI creatives? I seriously doubt it. If we want to write the next "Write the future," we can't let Jerry Seinfeld be right when he said, "We're smart enough to invent AI, dumb enough to need it, and still so stupid we're not sure if we did the right thing." We have to prove we are smart enough to know if we did the right thing by not doing the wrong thing. The way to not hate knowing where all of the AI madness is going is to grab the prompts by the horns and shape AI as a tool, not as a *fait accompli*.

How not to hate AI being everywhere, all the time

The quick answer to this question is don't go to the Consumer Electronics Show (C.E.S.) in Las Vegas. I went in January 2025, and it seemed like they were pumping AI into the oxygen they pump into the casinos. The event could've easily been renamed C-AI-S and no one would've batted an A or an I. Considering the conference is all about the next, wildest technology in the world, that makes sense. But do I really need to hear about AI when I'm at the grocery store?

Once again, Jeff Kling captures the point from a slightly different angle.

I'm not a Luddite, but I'm wary of too much enthusiasm in any direction. If people are just a little too excited and in excess of evidence for that excitement, I go right to suspecting them of some motive, some agenda.

It's true that AI is the world's best tech multi-tool, but I don't think it needs to be mandatory for every single step of the process. For example, we don't need to add Claude to all meetings. Sometimes, he should be marked "optional."

The best way I've found to not feel completely overwhelmed with AI all the time is to incorporate AI into your everyday routine. Have it read your TV scripts to see if another spot has been done like that in the past. Have it read your headlines to offer fresh ways in. Use it as a better Google. Make it create a workout plan for you. If this sounds counterintuitive, it's not. The more you use it, the less daunting it will feel and the more you'll understand when you should or shouldn't be considering it for any given project. So the answer to how not to hate being bombarded by AI every day is to use AI every day.

Advertising is dead. Long live advertising!

I was talking to Pancho Gonzalez, CCO/Founder at Inbrax in Chile. He said something that I thought was a perfectly simple summation of something as complex as AI and how creatives should think about the implications it has on the industry and the world. He said, "The moment you lose curiosity, you're done." That's AI in a nutshell. If you are operating out of fear, instead of curiosity, you're on the wrong path. But, if you're able to block all that out – the noise, the fear, the anxiety, the expectations, and race to the who knows where – then this new shiny object comes down to the same thing required for anyone to succeed in advertising – a curious mind.

Samira Ansari said it, too, when I asked her what it takes to succeed, and be happy in this business. "You have to be annoyingly curious." Scott Goodson echoed the sentiment, "I've always been curious. You have to be willing to try new things. No one can work if the sword of Damocles is hanging over your head. If you're afraid to make a mistake, forget it."

Ricardo Viramontes (AirBnB, SpringHill, Apple, Lyft, CAA, W+K), CCO/Art Director, stressed not just curiosity, urgency.

> You have to embrace it, period. Fully. You will not evolve and you will be left behind. It's part of your job. How can I add (this new tech) to my arsenal? I'm a storyteller, problem solver and creative, why wouldn't I want these technologies? How will it affect my work? The onus is on us to be proactive in our future.

So maybe that's how we learn not to hate the shiny new object – whether AI or any other future tool. Approach it with curiosity and urgency, not animosity or fear. I asked ChatGPT what it thought about this approach.

This is what it said:

I think that's a wise and open-minded approach. Fear and resistance often come from the unknown, but curiosity allows us to explore new possibilities, understand the nuances, and shape technology to serve us better. AI, like any tool, is neither inherently good nor bad—it's how we use it that matters.

Of course, healthy skepticism is important, too. Not every shiny new thing is beneficial, and it's fair to ask tough questions. But if we approach innovation with curiosity rather than animosity, we give ourselves the best chance to harness its potential while keeping its risks in check.

What sparked this thought for you?

Come on, GPT. Read the room.

Note

1 "A Conversation with Bing's Chatbot Left Me Deeply Unsettled". Kevin Roose. *The New York Times*. February 17, 2023.

Chapter 10

How not to hate awards

I don't love awards. I don't quite hate them, I just kinda hate them. Not the awards themselves, but the culture, the expectation, and the pressure. I hate the all-or-nothing mentality. So, this is a tricky chapter to write when I need help tamping down the hate myself.

I know what you're thinking, "He kinda hates awards because he hasn't won enough of them." That may be right, but you'd have to ask my therapist and he'd probably go on about how all-or-nothing thinking is linked to anxiety and unrealistic expectations, which leads to depression and so on. Plus, he's not cheap. So maybe take my word for it that you'd only be partly right. I have won my fair share of awards, but not nearly the haul that some industry titans have amassed. Yet, that's not why I kinda hate awards. I have many more reasons. And you're gonna hear about them! Because, hey, we're gonna work through this one together.

> I love that I get to see the best thinking in our industry through awards. I love that ideas I see still make me jealous. I love that it pushes me as a creative to always think beyond what we believe is possible. I truly love that the right ideas can make a real difference to brands. Big ideas for brands that bring in results—what's not to like about that?
> —Samira Ansari, CCO (Ogilvy, Deutsch, FCB)

Reason #1 I kinda hate awards: they're never enough

I kinda hate awards because even when you win them, they're not enough. Sure, it feels really good at first. You're relieved, exhilarated, validated. You won! They get it! The hard work was worth it! You post about it. Snap selfies with your award. You get lots of praise and comments. But like any high, there's also a hangover. And once that hits you, the dread sets in. Because the pressure to do it again next year begins…immediately.

Congratulations! *You suck.*

You won silver?

Great! Now win gold.

DOI: 10.4324/9781032615707-10

You won gold?
Great! Win Titanium.
You won Titanium?

How not to hate starting all over again

Mike Byrne, Founding Partner/Global Creative Officer of Anomaly, sees the chance to create again as what he loves about the business, despite the pressure. In a LinkedIn post posted the day after the Super Bowl, he describes the thrill of the unknown, which also applies to the yearly awards grind. "The cursor blinks staring back at you. And all you can do is focus on what's next, what's in front of you. Thinking of all the wonderful possibilities out there. Damn, I love this business."

The slate is clean, the page is blank, and the clock is ticking. So how do you go about revving the engine back up again?

Start building next year's submissions now

An agency where I used to work started a really smart and aggressive approach to awards one year, right after we didn't win at Cannes. Now I'm totally going to share that strategy with all of you (sorry guys). Like many agencies, we were always scrambling to pull together case studies and written submissions before the deadline. Everyone was swamped with client work, and not prioritizing the submissions until...UH OH! They're due next week! We would pay for extensions, then begging for one or two more days past that. It's a terrible way to try and craft your best argument. Here's what we did, and you can, too.

Create an awards committee and case study meeting

The most senior creative leadership would meet once a week and talk about which projects in the agency had awards potential. We would then invite the creative leads for those projects to present the ideas to the committee. Together, we would help push the ideas to maximize their impact. If there weren't any obvious projects worth the time, we would find a brief to push on. Once an idea got to a place we liked, we would start crafting the case study with the creative leads. This was a separate meeting, directly after the awards committee. Rather than waiting to make the work and then create the case, we would get ahead of it and adjust as we went.

Identify winnable categories

Cannes is over? Great. Now go watch all the Cannes work. And the One Show, while you're at it. Plus, the Andy's, Clios, D&AD, Emmy's, AICP, etc. Study what won and in what categories. Pay particular attention to the obscure categories. Can you beat the best retail idea? What about Direct? Or radio? Everyone wants to win in film, but would you rather be competing against Scorcese or Fincher for that? Or against some regional digital agency from Aarhus, Denmark in Creative Data? Because guess what? A gold Lion for the film looks the same as a gold Lion for Creative Data, OOH, or PR. A win is a win. If your work has the film chops. Aim for that. If you can diversify and take down some other category with less competition, do it. Or brief now so that you can. You've got a year. And the clock is ticking. Ugh, I kinda hate awards.

Put your eggs into a lot of different baskets

Entering awards shows is expensive, so this tip may not work for all. But I am also here to say, Cannes is not the only awards show that matters. I know in some countries that might get me struck by lightning, but it's true. It just depends on your goals, budget, and client demands. Do you want to win a few big awards on the global stage? Or do you want to win at a bunch of shows? National shows? Regional or state shows? What do you want the press release to be?

Obviously, everyone wants this one:

"Super Cool Agency wins highest award on biggest global stage"
Or...
"Super Cool Agency wins tons of awards at one big global show."

But these aren't bad either:

"Area Agency wins like 25 awards at a bunch of different awards shows"
Or, even...
"Area Agency has most winningest year ever at global, national and
    regional awards shows"
"My advice about awards is, enter everything you think you have a chance to win," says Grant Smith (Rise and Shine and partners, Yamamoto, McCann, BBDO), CCO/Writer. So, if you if you did a super good ad or campaign for a medical supply warehouse, and it you know that the category is going to be full of really big name and recognized competition that produced amazing things in Cannes but that there's some regional

award show where the competition is maybe a little bit less. Go for the trophy. And focus your efforts towards what you think can win. And if you think you can win, go all in.

—Grant Smith's advice (Rise and Shine and partners, Yamamoto, McCann, BBDO), CCO/Writer.

Don't hope you win. Plan to win

Make the case studies real internal projects

Instead of an add-on, the projects had real resources and timelines. Teams were responsible for advancing them just like client work. Make it real and people accountable, and it will happen. On time and on budget. And you'll like it a lot more than when you scramble.

Get a real production budget approved by a real CFO

To craft an amazing case study takes more than amazing work. It takes a production of its own. Get a budget for an editor, maybe even some additional filming if needed. You'll want to make the story of the idea even more amazing than the idea, and that takes a script, production, and post-production resources and time. Which, again, is never on your side.

Rally everyone internally

This doesn't work if it's a purely creative exercise. You need all departments in lockstep. That means, making sure Account communicates with the client, in case we need their support. It means strategy, so they're involved in the framing and even research if you need more context. Project management so they can make this a real project and not an afterthought. Production because, well, didn't you just read the previous paragraph? The CFO because, didn't you just read the paragraph before that? Come on. Pay attention.

Tell your clients to save their money

Not to spend on submissions, but to save up for proactive ideas. The stuff outside the scope and not officially briefed. The back of the book ideas. The work that you'll love making together and will make you both famous. The planned, briefed work should have your attention, sure. That may even be the award-winning stuff. If so, great. But you need more money on the table, irons in the fire, or skin in the game. Pick your cliché. Get a budget approved for work they can't plan for or know what to expect. Once you have it, everyone will want to make the most of it.

Reason #2 I kinda hate awards: they shouldn't matter

Think about it. We work in an industry that awards ourselves for ideas we get paid to create for clients to sell their products to customers. Shouldn't the sales of those products be rewarding enough? Or the signing of a larger scope the next year because they're so happy with your work? Or shouldn't it be enough if your ideas are talked about in culture? Or mocked on SNL? Turns out, nope. We need trophies, too.

Do we need another hero? Yes, it seems we do

You know who deserves an award probably more than the team that works on the McDonald's account? The Employee of the Month at the McDonald's in Wichita who dropped in a custom batch of fries during the dinner rush, just to satisfy your "not too salty" request, and then cleaned them off the floor after your four-year-old threw a tantrum because they weren't salty enough. Now THAT guy/girl/whomever deserves a trip to the South of France for a week.

But do we? It's debatable. Kidding. It's not. That yacht has sailed. We need trophies. As Grant Smith put it, ever so bluntly, "We shouldn't have to participate in this. The whole thing is unfair. The problem is, unless you're there, and unless you're part of it, you run the risk of seeming irrelevant." And that's the rub. We need awards because we say we need them. And therefore, that need must be fulfilled. Or we might be that toddler throwing fries on the floor. See you on La Croissette, I guess.

How not to hate the fact that you have to compete for awards

1 You'll get a case study out of it, even if you don't win.
2 You get to go to a fun party, even if you lose.
3 Your clients will get to go to the party, too. Which is good for you and the agency.
4 Hey, you might win! (But, see above).
5 Every award on your resume means more $ on your salary eventually. (Cha-ching!)
6 Your mom will be even more proud of you.

Wow, this self-therapy thing is weirdly helpful. You know what may make you and me feel even better? Next time you're feeling bad about not having won a Lion, either this year or ever in your career, consider this. The following actors and actresses have *never won an Academy Award:*

Tom Cruise
Robert Downey Jr.
Samuel L. Jackson
Glenn Close
Amy Adams
Bill Murray
Stanley Tucci
Edward Norton
Michelle Williams
Johnny Depp
Sigourney Weaver
John Goodman
Angela Bassett
Jim Carrey
Woody Harrelson
Annette Benning
Liam Neeson
Michel Pfieffer
Ian McKellen
Ralph Fiennes

These are some of the biggest names in Hollywood who have made some of the greatest movies of all time. In fact, as of January 2025, Samuel L. Jackson was the highest-grossing leading actor in the US and Canada, with movies featuring him as protagonist making $5.85 billion at the North American box office. Robert Downey Jr. came in second with $5.47 billion.[1] Do you care that they've never won their industry's biggest award? Or do you just love their work?

This helps me quite a bit. It's a reminder that you can enjoy a very successful and satisfying career without winning the industry's biggest trophies.

Winning isn't everything. But it's not nothing

Do you need a big, huge fancy job to win awards or have a client care? Well, no. But winning a bunch of awards can create both of those situations. Leaders in the C-suite at the world's biggest brands care a lot about awards. And from the outside, awards signal what you can do for their business. Plus, let's face it. People like winners, and if you're a winner, then that winning can rub off on those around you. It also makes your clients look good, and that's good for everyone.

Consider this perspective from Christian McMahan, former CMO of Heineken USA,

> One thing people underestimate is how awards can serve as a tool to help clients defend their agency choices to other internal stakeholders. Everyone wants to be with a winner. In the absence of experience or the depth of knowledge to rationalize a choice, knowing that an agency has been consistently recognized for the quality of their work can be an important data point that some clients rely on in their decision-making process.[2]

I wrote the following headline for a Nike campaign about the attitude of a New York baseball fan, which could just as easily sum up the feeling of awards season (Figure 10.1).

Or consider the perspective of Camilo Ruano (Ogilvy, DDB, Pereira O'Dell), a Colombian-born CD/Art Director, living and working in the US since 2019. Talking about the importance of awards to him and his partner, Ivan Rivera (Ogilvy, DDB, Pereira O'Dell). "We are here because of awards. It's the way we demonstrate to the US government that we are talented people…and to come here to work in the US." Ivan added to his point. Even before moving to the US to work at Pereira O'Dell, he saw an even more fundamental life benefit of awards. "I got my first apartment and my independence for my mother's home thanks to one award."

Camilo then put it in a way that resonated with the soccer fan in me, by comparing the winning of an award to winning at the end of the season. "Winning an award is like winning a tournament. Soccer players work to win a tournament at the end of the year. That's the purpose." Great point. No one plays in the Champions League to be happy with how they played each 90-minute match. They want to hoist up the trophy and jump up and down on the stage, while confetti rains down.

So, fine. It's not fair for me, or anyone else in the business, to hate on awards and say they don't matter when they do, a lot, to many people – creatives,

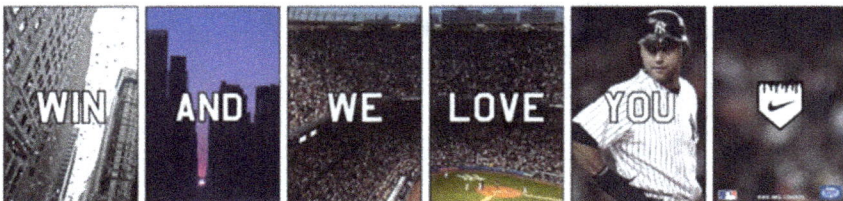

Figure 10.1 A headline for Nike baseball that could just as easily be about advertising awards season. Courtesy of the author.

agencies, clients, and brands. So if we accept that awards do matter, then so does learning how to win them.

Like Matt Damon's character Mike McDermott in the movie *Rounders* said, "Why do you think the same five guys make it to the final table of the World Series of Poker every year? What, are they the luckiest guys in Las Vegas? It's a skill game."

Winning isn't luck. It's preparation, repetition, and don't-screw-this-up-tion

There are also a lot of techniques you can use to give yourself the best chance to win. The first and possibly most important one is how you craft your case study. Watch all of the Cannes awards-winning case studies each year to see what worked – via the official site, or if you don't want to pay the steep price, go to lovetheworkmore.com.

Years ago, I asked PJ Pereira to give a presentation to the Pereira O'Dell creative department called, "The Art of the Case Study." After countless hours of judging awards shows, he broke down the way 90% of the case studies were created (ask PJ, it's his lesson, not mine). They all had the same formula. It was kind of hard to watch case studies after that presentation. They all seemed so cliché. But as with any cliché, they're like that for a reason – it works.

Reason #3 I kinda hate awards: when they're a distraction

If it is declared from the beginning of the project that the sole purpose of that assignment is to win an award, you've likely already lost. When you're being asked to win an award, you're no longer trying to solve a problem. You're trying to win a trophy. You'll see this kind of provocation all the time in creative briefs. It's meant to inspire, to give you permission to go for it and "Swing for the fences! No idea is too big! Free yourself from the shackles of mediocrity!" But what it actually does, is quite the opposite. Camilo Ruano said, "When that happens, you're taking away all the fun of the brief." And he's right. That kind of provocation makes creatives tense up and freak out. Ambition is great. Inspiration is great. Titanium expectations are not. At least not at the outset.

Greg Hahn, co-founder and CCO of Mischief @No Fixed Address agrees,

Mentally, awards can take a toll. Know that it more often feels worse to lose than it does better to win. But also understand nobody is paying attention to your awards count more than you. So don't focus too much on not winning. Focus on making work you love.

In other words, don't let awards distract you from a great idea. But once you do have an idea that has clear award-winning potential, *that's* the time to pour on the pressure. That's when you put everything you got into making sure that idea makes it to the finals and takes home the hardware. Protect it. Obsess over it. Write and rewrite the case study until it's perfect. Same with the written entry. Craft. Hone. And don't forget to proofread.

Judge. Jury. And validation-er

So why do we put ourselves through this, year in and year out? The more creatives I asked, the more they said the same thing: validation. Anjali Rao, CD/Copywriter said,

> We all want to feel like what we're doing means something even when we are just selling fried chicken or cookie dough. So when you get an award, it's like, 'Okay, now I feel like I've left my mark on the world and somebody has given me a trophy so they also agree.

Greg Hahn said something similar,

> Because this is a subjective business and an awarded piece of work in your book will have some validation by others that it's good. It will also help you stand out in a sea of portfolios of work that people aren't familiar with.

Camilo Ruano jumped in with the same thought around validation, "More than the ego, an award is something to let everyone else know your work has value."

We want to know that our ideas are as good as we think they are, and we want other creatives to tell us that they agree. It's as simple as that. And I think that's an explanation I can live with.

Do I still kinda hate awards? Only when I don't win

Hopefully, this chapter helped some of the haters out there. It helped me, a little. Just reframing the pressure, expectations, and emotional rollercoaster that is awards season makes it a little easier to stomach. Instead of focusing on the pressure, focus on the idea. Instead of trying to force a win, focus on the categories where you can be successful. Instead of leaving things to chance, craft your case study.

And when you win, enjoy it. Otherwise, what's the point?

Notes

1 Highest-grossing leading actors of all time in the United States and Canada as of January 2025, by cumulative domestic box office revenue. Statista.com. Laura Carollo. January 6, 2025.
2 Does the Cannes Festival of Creativity Matter? Forbes.com. MarketShare. Scott Goodson. June 18, 2013.

Chapter 11

How not to hate yoga and tofu

Advertising can be really fun, despite what the title of this book suggests. I'm talking about the non-working stuff now: the happy hours, indulgent breakfasts, free pizza, the $30 salads at an edit, global travel, nice hotels, and decadent client dinners. It's about time we talked about the good stuff. THIS IS WHAT YOU SIGNED UP FOR!!! WORKING LATE ON YOUR BIRTHDAY IS FINALLY GONNA PAY OFF!

SFX: Bubble bursts

The business can also be relentless when you combine all of the above scenarios with back-to-back Zooms/Teams/BlueJeans calls, insane time-lines, fire drill pitches, and weekend briefings. We all know that Diet Coke at 3 am feeling, and it's not a good one. If you don't take care of yourself, no one else will.

Remember those rejuvenating mental health days we all got off during COVID? Those were cute. Now that those mental health days are mostly a thing of the past and the grind is grinding you up again, you better check yourself before you wreck yourself. You can't wait for your boss or agency to tell you to take a day, because by then it's too late. Drink before you're thirsty, as we say in cycling.

How not to hate sliding into an unhealthy cycle of unhealthiness from too much advertising

Rule #1: put yourself first

I know, I know…it's not up to you most of the time. People are putting you on a million briefs and triple-booking your calendar. It can be hard to know when to raise the white flag. I didn't figure out how to do it until I became an ECD and PJ Pereira, Co-Founder/Creative Chairman of Pereira O'Dell, pulled me aside to urge me to take time for myself. As I recall, PJ said something like, "Nick is the most important brand at the agency and if Nick isn't in a good place, then the other brands won't be either."

DOI: 10.4324/9781032615707-11

That advice smacked me upside the head, but not right away. I immediately went back to killing myself day and night, eating and drinking poorly, not getting enough sleep or exercise. But I'm here to say, that was dumb. Do yourself a favor, sooner than later. Because this attention to your health is just as important to sustaining a long, successful career as winning a bunch of awards.

My current boss Scott Goodson, CEO/Co-Founder of StrawberryFrog, said the same thing,

> You've got to take care of yourself. It's a stressful job, and you're constantly giving all of yourself. It's like being an actor every night on Broadway, going out and pounding the stage and giving your full heart out. It's very draining, you (need to) go for a walk, or do yoga, or do cooking, go to a museum or go to Sicily, whatever.

I am obviously not a professional personal trainer, nutritionist, dietician, doctor, nurse practitioner, or any other kind of medical practitioner on mental or physical health and well-being. I've worked on healthcare brands, but that doesn't count. Then again, the same could be said for half of the influencers on TikTok and people believe those kooks, so.

I'm just a 40-something-year-old dude who's put myself through the ringer for decades and finally somehow managed to figure out how to balance work with working out (most of the time). That said, don't sue me if you don't lose 25 lbs. in 25 days using this unscientifically unproven method that isn't really a method at all or intended to set you on a path of fitness nirvana. This chapter is merely a reality check on work/life balance. But hey, if you do manage to lose some weight and/or clear up your mental health forever, then great! *GO TELL YOUR FRIENDS TO BUY THIS BOOK.*

Good habits. Good creativity

Here are some completely obvious, good-for-you habits that will actually help creativity (and probably other things too). A healthy mind and body = better creative ideas, simple as that. If you can't think straight, you can't think great. That's what I always say. And by always I mean, I just made that up and it sounds kinda slogan-y and memorable so I'm leaving it in.

Here's that unprofessional, unscientifically tested part:

Wake up!

Early. Start with 7 am. Then try 6:30 am. Earlier if you can handle it. There's a whole book dedicated to this approach called *The 5 am Club* by Robin Sharma. But this is advertising and if you're up at 5 am, you're probably on a pitch. So again, start with 7 am. That's a nice time if there ever was one.

You can go work out or just drink coffee. The key is to get up. Start your metabolism and your mind grapes. Try it twice a week. Set an alarm. It'll pay off later in the day. Concepting sessions will be easier. Meetings will be smoother. Internals, less interal-y. Then you'll get tired and go to bed earlier. Then get up easier tomorrow. A non-vicious cycle.

Move your ass

And your arms and legs. According to a 2021 study quoted in *The NY Times*, activity and creativity are linked. That article asked the question, "Can Exercise Make You More Creative?"[1] The answer, it turns out, is absolutely. It says "Our brains change in response to physical activity, in part because during exercise we marinate our brains with extra blood, oxygen and nutrients." And "active imaginations start with active lives." But don't take it from me. I'm just a writer who found an article you didn't know existed to make a point you may have already assumed was correct. So, good for you. Now go take your dog for a walk. Or do some downward dog.

Eat Tofu. Or something like it

Jeez, this is starting to read like a middle school health class, right? Get more sleep! Exercise! Eat better! Thanks for the earth-shattering insights, Nick! Well, turns out your middle school health teacher was right. If you want another smart sounding source, the Harvard Health Blog says "Multiple studies have found a correlation between a diet high in refined sugars and impaired brain function." Harvard? Oof. I thought this book was supposed to be fun? But wait, there's more! It goes on to say, "Like an expensive car, your brain functions best when it gets only premium fuel."[2] Premium fuel? Sounds like an Exxon brief. Understand now? The point is, eat better = think better. Don't like tofu? Fine. Get a salad.

Play a guitar

Or piano. Or violin. Or go draw. Or paint. Or garden. Or do a crossword. No, not the crossword app on your phone. You'll end up checking email. Go wake up another part of your brain and give the advertising part of it a rest. Yes, your brilliant mind can get tired of having all those Titanium-winning ideas all the time. Even Schwarzenegger puts down the dumbbells every once in a while and reads a book.

Read a screenplay

This isn't just for writers. Art directors, I'm looking at you, too. A well-written screenplay is a masterclass in storytelling on a page. A great screenplay reads as if you are watching it. Actually better, since it doesn't have a camera, actors or music. Scene descriptions must be sharp and concise. Dialogue, natural, and moving. The world must be clear and evocative. The pages must be oozing with emotion. Every word on every page is important. Want to help your own creative process? Study screenplays as much as Cannes case studies.

Clear your inbox

Yes, I'm one of those people. Follow me to freedom. Zero it out. You can do it. You should do it. Your mind (and mom) will thank you. I know this is a controversial and polarizing POV. Like choosing the British *Office* TV series over the American *Office* TV series. If you can't let go, flag the messages you need to revisit. A red flag is better than a red dot. A flag is a reminder. A dot is a roadblock.

If you don't want to do all of the above, there's one thing that will help you most of all...

Get some sleep

Ok, now this really does sound like an annoying lesson in the obvious. But seriously, sleep is the single most important aid to creativity. Thomas Edison famously thought sleep was a waste of time. He napped instead, holding weighted balls in each hand so that when he started to drift off he would drop the balls, and wake up. He did this because that moment of sleep onset is said to trigger creative thoughts.[3] But until you invent the next lightbulb, get some real rest.

Kurt Lenard used to take legit naps between an editor sharing a cut, and addressing our notes. That was pro-level sleeping skills. He could literally tilt his head back, close his eyes, and within seconds, be snoring. To be clear, this was not 1944. We were not sitting back-to-back in a trench in Normandy. We were at Mackcut, probably working on some ESPN spots. But I don't know how he did it.

Assuming you do some of the things above, but can't actually sleep at work – how can you avoid hating what advertising is doing to your mind, body, and soul?

Rule #2: protect your time during the work day

You don't want to take care of yourself outside of work? Your choice. I am not exactly a model citizen for good, clean living. But I am an advocate for one very important part of your work day: being a ruthless guard dog with your calendar. You don't need an Executive Assistant to protect your time like you have the Secret Service on the payroll. You just have to get into the practice of doing it yourself.

Learn your ABCs: always busy calendar

Drop a block on your calendar and label it as "busy." Who can argue with that? You are busy being not busy, which is the best way to help you once you do get really busy. Don't wait until the day of. Check your calendar a day or two in advance. Once you see it start to fill up, send out the advance team (still sticking with the Secret Service analogy here), and throw down some yellow caution tape, big orange cones, a metaphorical protective perimeter of dudes in dark suits, black sunglasses, and ear-pieces. You need protection from assault because meetings are an assault on your time and creative capacity. But don't go overboard. You'll get found out. People will stop respecting your "busy" blocks and expose you for the calendar con man (or woman) you are. Be careful out there. Stay frosty.

As you climb the creative ladder – or as we all still learn to work in this hybrid environment – your days will be filled with nothing but meetings. It's hell. Sure, you like almost everyone in those meetings and the conversations are important, but it's still hell. If you don't schedule time to go to the bathroom, or make a tuna Niçoise salad, or stretch your hammies, someone will definitely slap a *Client status 2.0 follow up to the presentation prep chem check download post mortem meeting* on your calendar faster than you can say, *I'm off camera but listening*.

Let's recap:

1 Don't let anyone push your calendar around like you're in a Matchbox Twenty song.
2 Avoid Matchbox Twenty references.
3 Throw "busy" (not actually busy) time on your calendar.
4 Thank me later.

So what do you do while you're busy not being busy? (P.S. If you have to put "busy" on your calendar on the weekend, see Chapters 5 or 12) Easy. Something else, preferably not advertising.

Rule #3: get rid of the guilt

We've clearly established that creative people need more sleep, more protected time, and less Matchbox Twenty references. So now that you're in the right frame of mind to save your mind from mindless meetings and creativity time-sucks, what should you do?

First, don't hate that you're lying.

Second, adopt the George Constanza philosophy that says, it's not a lie if you believe it.

Finally, ditch any feelings of guilt because not being busy is actually part of the job.

How not to hate that you're lying about being "busy" because you're still being productive

When I asked the famously pro-level napper, Kurt Lenard what he does to take his mind off a project, "Sleep. Eat. Nap. Turn off. Do anything but ads or think." Sleep was literally 50% of the advice. Here's some ideas for the other 50% of the time, for those who may want to be a bit more productive.

Don't nap, like Kurt. Give Kurt a call. Sleep is important (duh), just not when you're trying to distract yourself from work. You'll probably dream about the problem you're trying to solve anyway, so it's not really an escape. Call a creative friend like Kurt, instead. Yes, that $1,000 computer in your hand also makes calls. Call and talk to your Kurt-like friend about stuff creative people talk about. You'll probably end up talking about advertising, but maybe your friend will say something that triggers a new thought. Or maybe he'll fall asleep halfway through the call. If so, that's on you.

Don't do laundry. This is not a Tide ad. Just pull out another black t-shirt. Laundry is not a hobby. Just ask the team that works on Tide. Laundry is a chore and while yes, a chore can take your mind off of things, you won't feel that satisfied once you get back into things. Your clothes will be brighter, but not your mind.

Draw the Metallica "Master of Puppets" album cover like you're 10 years old again. (Just me?) Or the Sonic Youth "Goo" album. Or the Sex Pistols logo. Or just that tree outside your window. Draw something. Anything. Even if you suck at drawing. Do as Kurt Vonnegut says,

> Practice any art, music, singing, dancing, acting, drawing, painting, sculpting, poetry, fiction, essays, reportage, no matter how well or badly, not to get money and fame, but to experience becoming, to find out what's inside you, to make your soul grow.

If you have 30 minutes, create something that wasn't there 30 minutes before you started, that no one controls but you.

Go to the movies. This is one of the biggest cliches in advertising, but it's cliche because it works. Just maybe check the runtime before you go, so you don't unwittingly commit yourself to a three-hour and 35-minute film like *The Brutalist* when you have a creative review at EOD.

Listen to a podcast. You're in advertising. I don't have to tell you what podcast to listen to. You're probably presenting an idea for a podcast tomorrow. But just a friendly reminder of how nothing takes your mind off a bank merger campaign quite like a triple homicide murder mystery.

Speaking of listening: Don't listen to me. This is your time to take care of your mental and physical health. Only you know how to do that best. But if you need a reminder, well here it is. If you need an actual calendar invite type reminder – then put down this book right now and put it in your phone, with alarm set to "at time of event" and repeat set to "daily."

Listen to Sir John Hegarty instead. In a LinkedIn post, he made "The creative case for bunking off" in which he said, "We glamorize grind. The 12-hour days. The 'always on' culture. The sleep-shaming and hustle worship. But creativity doesn't work like that. The mind needs space. And boredom. And rest. To wander, to play, to imagine." He also referenced how Darwin "bunked off twice a day. For a long, solitary stroll down a gravel track near his home in Kent. That's when the ideas came." So again, don't take it from me. Take it from the H in BBH, and Charles Darwin.

Whether you listen to this advice or not, I'll never know. And I can't claim to be the poster child for health myself. But I think about it a lot, and try to keep the balance. But I also know that nobody gets into advertising because they value their physical and mental health above all other things. We get into advertising because we like to get paid to be creative and like having our mom call us up and ask, "Was that your Pedigree dog commercial I saw during *SNL*?" Make your mom proud. Stop killing yourself. It's only advertising. I'm Captain Obvious and I approve this message.

HATE LESS BEFORE NOON THAN MOST PEOPLE HATE ALL DAY

Designer: Bryan Haker

Notes

1 "Can Exercise Make You More Creative? Gretchen Reynolds". *The NY Times.* February 3, 2021.
2 "Nutritional Psychiatry: Your Brain on Food. Eva Selhub MD". *Harvard Health Blog.* September 18, 2022.
3 "Sleep onset is a creative sweet spot". Célia Lacaux, Thomas Andrillon, Céleste Bastoul, Alexandrine Fonteix-Galet, Yannis Idir, Isabelle Arnulf, and Delphine Oudiette. *Science Advances.* December 8, 2021.

Chapter 12

How not to hate other random stuff you never thought you'd hate about advertising

Advertising is a hard business. Maybe not compared to a disaster relief coordinator or porta-potty repairman, but it is still hard. For an industry built on convincing people to love feeling like a winner or just love leather seats, there's plenty of hate to go around. Way more than can fit neatly into chapters, it turns out. To pitch this book, I had to present my editor with a table of contents and chapter summary. This meant I needed a pretty good idea going into the writing of all the points I wanted to hit. As I started interviewing creatives and writing the main contents of each chapter, so many topics came up that fell outside the outline. Hence this catchall chapter of random stuff.

How not to hate feeling like you're on call 24/7

You're not a trauma surgeon, even though it can feel like it sometimes. The higher you climb up the ladder, the earlier and later the texts will come. Unlike trauma surgery, it's not usually about the urgency of the matter so much as the anxiety of the person calling.

When your boss, account director, or managing director, inevitably texts you at 7:30 am or 11:30 pm, you can learn not to hate this by doing the following:

Uncheck "Send Read Receipts" on your phone. They won't know you saw their message. Too late for that? Then try one of these replies:

"Got it. Will give it a think." – because you will, just not now.
"On it." – but offer no timeline
"On it. Tomorrow ok?" – buy yourself some time
"Great idea!" – and leave it at that

They just want to know that you saw and are planning to address the request. If the text is from Account or Strat, the above replies work. But

DOI: 10.4324/9781032615707-12

so does…"Kk" (but not "k," right kids?) or "Leave it with me" or just not replying at all. It's late/early, after all.

If they persist, it may actually be urgent. If they don't, the issue will probably work itself out. Or can wait till tomorrow. My bet is on the latter. You can also send a "You got it dude" type meme gif, just to let them know how much you appreciate a text way out of working hours. But your mileage may vary there.

A sure fire way to make the texts stop is to call them. Yes, an actual phone call. Believe me. They don't want to talk at 7:30 am or 11:30 pm, that's why they texted. But if you don't want to get in a back and forth, a quick call (answered or not) will end it, right then and there.

How not to hate being briefed at 5 pm on a Friday to turn around work by Monday at 10 am

In a LinkedIn post, Eric Segal, Founder X&O, Chief Creative Officer wrote, "Weekend work isn't a badge of honor. It's a sign of a broken system." I wholeheartedly agree with this, but sometimes it's unavoidable. When it happens, you can chug on a bottle of Hater-ade or you can get over it and get to work.

Rob Munk (Arts & Letters, BBDO, W+K), CD/Writer, actually enjoys what most people hate.

> Even though everybody hates getting briefed on a Friday, I like getting briefed on a Friday because it gives me the weekend to have something to think about in the back of my mind. I guess I like thinking about how to solve these problems.

If you're like Rob, then this section may not be for you. If you're like Eric Segal, then let's dive in.

First of all, breathe. Again, it's only advertising. A Friday evening briefing is not anyone's favorite place to find themselves. Maybe you had big plans on Saturday. Or Sun-

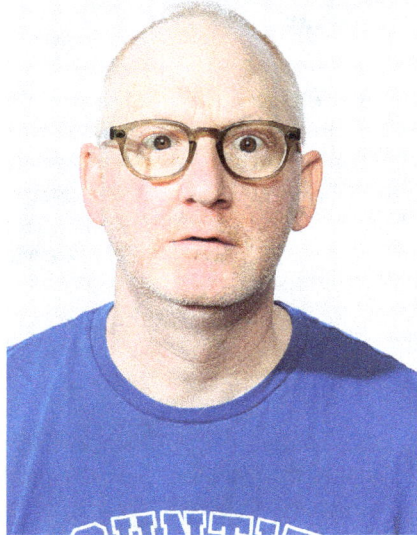

Figure 12.1 Rob Munk. CD, Writer.

day. Maybe those big plans are just sleeping in. Whatever the case, you're going to be in this situation if you work in advertising. But there are silver linings, or at least ways to relieve the overall frustration in this predicament. Look at it this way. This is a desperation briefing. And you know what desperate times call for, right? Reaching into your external hard drive of killed ideas for unrelated clients from your time at various different agencies, and trying to fit them to whatever this fire drill brief is about. That's what you were thinking, right? Don't worry. We all do it. And it's okay. Many of your favorite campaigns were probably presented and rejected by one brand, only to live another life for something completely different. I know a few, but won't rat those creatives/agencies out.

If recycling ideas isn't your thing, or you've tried it already before with little success, fret not. The other silver lining to the Friday late afternoon/early evening emergency briefing is that *SOMETHING* is going to get presented to clients on Monday. So go crazy. Pull out the wildest ideas you've always wanted to present. Dream bigger than big. You still have to make it make sense. And you should probably also temper your ideas with a buyable option. But don't hold back the crazy stuff. Embrace them. You never know. The agency might just buy one. The client might just buy one. And desperation may lead to inspiration. Or at least the guts to say "Screw it, let's do it."

How not to hate yourself halfway through a presentation at McDonald's corporate headquarters

There I was, McDonald's HQ in Chicago, two weeks into my new job at Translation, about to present some fun TVC scripts to sell the new McDonald's Crispy Chicken Bacon Clubhouse Sandwich. I was seated across a table way too tiny to be taken seriously, across from clients I'd never met, with new colleagues I barely knew. But the lesson isn't about the tiny table. It's about how you should never eat McDonald's right before you present ideas to McDonald's, even if you're at McDonald's HQ. I learned this lesson so you don't have to.

I'd been working on the Chicken Clubhouse brief for a few weeks, gearing up for this big presentation, but hadn't tried the sandwich yet. So I thought,

I know I've been up since 4:45am and my stomach is already a little queasy from taking the 6am flight to O'Hare. And I know McDonald's may not be the best first meal option for me right now, but they just switched over from breakfast to lunch, and the Premium Crispy Chicken Bacon Clubhouse Sandwich is on the menu, so I should try it, right? I mean, I'm in McDonald's HQ, so theoretically this should be the best version of this sandwich anywhere.

So yes, I ordered one, with bacon, fries, and a soda because – I mean, when in Rome, right? I scarfed down the sandwich, fries, and soda in the five minutes we had before heading upstairs. It's worth noting that no one else I traveled with ate anything. They knew better. They've been here before. #rookiemistake

Cut to the tiny table I mentioned earlier. We do our intros, Account sets the stage, Strat recaps the brief, and then kicks it over to me. Oh, but not before the lead account guy announces he's going to record the meeting to help with notes.

Did I mention four out of the five scripts I was there to present were songs? Not jingles. Full on, 30-second joke-filled songs, that I now had to perform with a belly full of fried chicken, reheated bacon, "premium" sauce, wilted lettuce, mealy tomato, sugary bun, crispy fries, and ice cold Coca-Cola – running around my stomach like it's an Escape Room with the walls closing in, desperately looking north *or* south for a way out.

Seven years later, I don't remember any of the scripts. But I do remember feeling like the sounds coming from inside my stomach were louder than my "singing" (they weren't), and that at any moment I could resemble Harry Dunne from *Dumb and Dumber*, sprinting urgently to find a bathroom door to lock (I didn't). The presentation didn't go well. Shocking, I know. The clients didn't buy any of the spots, and I must've been asked off the business because that was the last McD's brief I saw. Fine by me. Lesson learned. Disaster avoided. That is, unless that voice memo is ever unearthed. Upshot is – don't wait to try the product until ten minutes before a presentation that requires you to "sing" a bunch of scripts. Unless the product is Jim Beam.

DON'T HATE THE SMALL STUFF UNLESS IT'S A 180x50 BANNER AD THEN GO AHEAD, HATE AWAY

Designer: Bryan Haker.

How not to hate reviewing a director's edit for the first time in front of them

If you love it, no problem. If you don't, just say it's "really interesting" a lot and then jump to a scene you have a small comment on. Nothing big like the opening shot. Try a nitpicky thing, like a facial expression. Don't bring up structure initially. That's too big of a deal. Aim lower, like the music. Or the placement of the VO. The director will probably lose interest and leave the room. Then, you can take over and do what you want. If they don't leave, ask "Did you try this?" a lot until they do. I hate even putting this down on paper because hopefully you're on the same page as the director, but if not, these tricks can work.

How not to hate feeling like your client is going to ruin the music in your commercial

First, remember, it's not "your" commercial. It's a commercial you presented to your client, who then got internal buy-in within her organization, approved your recommended director, paid for your flight and hotel room, slugged it out with you at the shoot, paid for the wrap party, and gave you the week you asked for to pull together an edit. It's her commercial, too. You may think you have better taste in music, and that may be true. But your client may be getting an earful about music from her boss, or just not be able to articulate what she wants in a track. Draw it out of her. Ask about the instruments, the build, the crescendo, the beat – music is hard to talk about, but don't give up.

There will be a song you'll agree on. It may not be that super obscure indie band from Akron you were hoping to introduce to the world. If that's the type of validation you seek, go work at a record label. If you want to align on a song that wins you favor with your client and gets you more approved work in the long run, you're better off listening to and entertaining her options. You may end up back where you started with your little Akron project, you may not. Music is really important. But it's also the most elusive part of the process. Go wide, try everything, and be open to anything.

How not to hate testing

Testing is every creative's worst enemy unless it goes well. Then, we love it. Ok, love is a strong word. We tolerate it. You'll never find a creative that actually likes testing. So how can you not hate it? This is a hard one. There's just so much to hate. It's such an unnatural way to present an idea to the world. Pay some random schmucks $50 to tell you what they think of an idea you haven't made yet? Aren't we the experts here? Yes, we are. But complaining about testing isn't going to make it go away. So let's try and be productive.

Lisa Preston (The New School, The Today Show, MTV), VP of Marketing, doesn't love testing either, but does find value in the insights gleaned from the process.

If you're going to a focus group to determine whether you should run this campaign or not, that's not going to work. Take it as directional and look at insights that you don't think you're getting. If you're talking about (the audience's) understanding of something, or if they bring some other insight by looking at the work, great. I shouldn't be written up in a report, as 'this is what we have to do.' But it should be like, 'Okay, that's, that's fodder for our further conversations.'

One way to hate testing less is to go to the testing. It will be torture, for sure. But at least you can put a face to the hate you're feeling when the results come back and take a big number two on your number one idea. When the results do come back, take a few deep breaths because you're going to need to make changes. Nothing survives testing unscathed. That said, unless the changes are foundational to the idea, you don't have to make them. Talk to the client about it. Say you'll keep these in mind when executing for real.

Of course, the best tactic to not hating testing is to not test the idea at all. Make the case to the client about why it's unnecessary. Tell them how really original, groundbreaking ideas don't need to be tested. They need to be watered and cared for. They need to be crafted and given the chance to be amazing. And they need to be a surprise. Reference agencies and campaigns that never went through testing, and never would've seen the light of day if they had. If none of this works, at the latest convince the clients that testing isn't a thumbs up, thumbs down proposition. We're here to listen and learn, not have creative be dictated by the results.

How not to hate going out to dinner with the client again

It's the end of a long week of prep for a shoot. You've been presenting casting and wardrobe all day. Some decisions went your way, some didn't. You have an inbox full of projects that need your attention. You're exhausted. You might even be jet-lagged. And the client wants to go to dinner. Again. Sorry, but you have to go. They won't remember the food, but they will remember you skipped dinner. This is the part of the business you can't learn in a portfolio school. You'll win more battles in post-production, or on future projects, with every client dinner you attend. It's not about the food. It's about being there, swapping stories, sharing hummus, deciding on sparkling or tap. If the client opts out for a night of room service, you're golden. If they ask if you want to grab sushi, the answer is, yes you do.

How not to hate presenting on three hours of sleep

It's going to happen at some point. Don't stress. This is when instinct takes over. And if you've been submerged in the project for weeks, you don't need as much prep as you think. One of the most valuable lessons I learned at times of being so incredibly strapped for time, and stretched so thin, is that the human brain is pretty unbelievable in times of stress. When you don't have the time or energy to overthink it, your brain will take over and just present it for you. It's kind of an out of body experience. You're running on fumes, yet the words are coming out beautifully. Rolling off your tongue. You're killing it. You don't know how, but you are. It's pure instinct. You're in the zone. But know that once you're done - get into an Uber immediately and go home. Or find a quiet room in the office. Because you're about the crash like nobody's business, in 3…2….1.

How to sum up a chapter about random hate

How can I sum up a chapter about all of the random things to hate in the advertising business? Why, with a famous song from one of the most famous ads ever Honda's "Grrr," of course. I think we all know how this one goes…

Can hate be good?
Can hate be great?
Can hate be good?
Can hate be great?
Can hate be something we don't hate?
Hate something
Change something
Hate something change something
Make something better.

You're welcome for the whistling earworm that will be now in your head for the rest of the day.

Chapter 13

How to be okay with hating advertising a little

For this final chapter, forget everything I've said up to this point. We heard back from the client and you're approved to throw some hate at advertising now. Shout, shout, let it all out. Because you can't get to a better place in your mind, body, and soul until you do. Yes, the entire premise of this book is to try and help you not hate the painful parts of this industry. But it's completely fine and entirely necessary to hate parts of advertising at times, so long as you ultimately love it in the end. A little bit of hate can help.

Let's say you hated being passed over for a Super Bowl brief one year, so you busted your ass and got it the next year. That's hate as motivation.

Or, imagine you hated how your CD killed your favorite idea – the one you were certain was the best and only answer – and that forced you to come up with another idea you love even more. That's properly channeled hate.

Or, what if you hated your job and that lit a fire in you to get a better one. And you got that better one. That's hate building a resume. No, a career.

As creatives, we need to keep hate somewhere in our toolbox. It helps us survive and thrive. We need that uncomfortable feeling when a brief doesn't seem right, or when an idea shouldn't be taking so long to crack. You need to hate losing in order to win. You need to hate how you present, in order to present better. You need to hate that feeling that things are going too smoothly, in order to see what you're missing. In order to learn and grow, you need to be able to hate any or all of the following, in order to turn them into a strength that makes you better at your job.

So go ahead. Hate…
8:30 am presentations
5:30 pm internals
Weekend work
Holiday work
Low budgets

DOI: 10.4324/9781032615707-13

No budgets
KPIs
Data
Radio
Banners
Programmatic
CRM
Client feedback on music
Client feedback on layouts
Client feedback on anything
Losing a pitch
Not winning at Cannes
Being a runner-up for an Emmy

And any of the million other things you can probably conjure up from your own experience.

Just don't let the hate consume you, ruin you, or make you cynical. That's the dangerous part. A healthy dose of skepticism is good. It's necessary and healthy. It can be powerful and help you keep the passion. It means you care enough to beat something up, to try and understand it or change it. Otherwise, you're taking the easy way out. Masking it with faux love or enthusiasm. Being a cog, not a creative. You need the hate to find the love.

If that doesn't work, and nothing else in this book helps, just remember:

It's only advertising.

Acknowledgments

First, I'd like to acknowledge that this book shouldn't have taken as long as it did to complete. I can still remember a conversation in 2023 with my editor Meredith Norwich, during which I foolishly declared that the book wouldn't take me that long because "I work in advertising, and we move fast." Little did I know two years would pass before handing in the final manuscript. Thank you to Meredith, her editorial assistant Bethany Nelson, and everyone at Taylor and Francis for your patience and guidance, as I finished the longest thing I've ever written.

Thank you, Robin Landa, Distinguished Professor at Kean University, for introducing me to Meredith and for raising the notion of writing a book like this in the first place. Thank you to Bryan Haker for your fun and memorable design contributions to the cover and "hate" mottos, you're an incredible designer and even better friend.

Thank you to all of the creative professionals who gave their time and insights and answered my various emails and requests. I am in awe of all the amazing minds I've had the pleasure to work with, alongside, and learn from over 23+ years in the business. And, of course, a huge thank you to Jeff Kling, a creative hero of mine, who agreed to write the foreword in less time than most advertising briefs.

Thank you to anyone who has asked about, offered advice on, or checked in on the progress of, as I complete this, my first book. Big shout-out to my good friend Jeremy Egner, who provided priceless advice, guidance, and encouragement to get me across the finish line. The friends I spend countless hours spinning around in circles with on the bike, who have been hearing about this book for years now. All of my colleagues at StrawberryFrog and client partners. My mother-in-law Sheila Isenberg, the esteemed author. My father-in-law Chris Collins, the poet and Renaissance man. You don't know how important all of your words of encouragement have been.

Thank you to the legends, fools, and trailblazers of this beautifully bizarre business, some who were mentioned in the text of this book, but many who were not. Without you wonderful weirdos and creatively fearless souls, I wouldn't have had the chance to create such a satisfying career, life, and 40,000+ word ode to the magic of what we do.

Thank you of course to those who gave me the fingers to write, the support to chase my advertising dream, and the courage to take on any challenge: my mom and dad, Cheryl Sonderup and Lee Sonderup. Also, my sister Tascha Nelson who I've always enjoyed sharing any and all advertising production stories, especially if they involve celebrities.

Finally, an immeasurable and full-hearted thank you to my lovely wife, Sunshine Flint, who gave me immense emotional support, the crucial time and space needed to write, and her expert editor's eye. Without all that, I may never have finished anything halfway decent. And to my two amazing daughters, Evie and Persey, for refilling my writer's tank with endless hugs. Dada's Saturdays are finally free once again.

About the author

Photograph by Andres Cevallos.

Nick Sonderup is an Emmy-nominated, globally awarded CCO with over 20 years of experience in advertising. His work has been recognized by nearly every industry awards show, including The Andys, One Show, Cannes Lions, Clios, D&AD, Effies, the ADC, and Campaign BIG awards. Nick has spent his career creating powerful, breakthrough work at many of the industry's most celebrated creative agencies for a wide range of clients. He is currently Co-CCO at StrawberryFrog, leading creative across multiple accounts, the creative department, and the StrawberryFrog brand.

Outside of agency life, Nick directed and starred in the film *100 Bands in 100 Days*, a Grand Jury award nominee at the 2010 SXSW Film Festival. He has also worked as an Adjunct Professor, teaching copywriting, and was a Co-Producer and CD of the Woodstock Comedy Festival. *How Not to Hate Advertising* is his first book. He lives in Brooklyn with his family.

Index

Note: *Italic* page numbers refer to figures.

For Product Safety Concerns and Information please contact our EU
representative GPSR@taylorandfrancis.com
Taylor & Francis Verlag GmbH, Kaufingerstraße 24, 80331 München, Germany